To Katie and Paul

Someday, when you are struggling or afraid, I
hope you'll hear my voice in these words.

Cover and formatting by:
Dave Zobel
DZOBEL Illustration

2015 by

Flying Feet Running Programs, LLC

Westminster, MD

dpgflyingfeet@aol.com

Printed and bound in the United States of America

First Printing 2015

Table of Contents

The beginning is often the end
And to make an end is to make a beginning.
The end is where we start from...
We shall not cease from exploration
And the end of all our exploring
Will be to arrive where we started
And know the place for the first time.

~ T. S. Eliot (Excerpt – "Little Gidding")

Preface

As I contemplated the layout for this book, I was continually reminded of a T. S. Eliot poem that I've read many times. It's inscribed on a monument on the campus of McDaniel College in Westminster, MD, and I always stop to read it when I pass.

"And the end of all our exploring will be to arrive where we started and know the place for the first time."

We all start in a beautiful place. I left that place, and I'm returning to it, through running. Your journey may be different, but I've come to believe that we will all pass through the same stages over the course of our lives –

Innocence, Fear, Struggle, Clarity and Peace.

It isn't always a linier process. The stages can blend together. There may be times when you are scared, you struggle and you gain some clarity all in the same day. But, at least for me, one stage has always been dominant, and this has been the sequence.

This book follows that progression. It tells of my running journey, but it also tells other running stories that I've observed or been told about first hand. As you read, you'll be taken through a process, a telling of a story about how running has helped me traverse the stages of life.

As I've written these words, they have guided me as I move toward the peace I've been searching for. Slowly but surely, I'm arriving at a place I love being.

It is my hope that these words can help guide you as well.

Introduction

Sometimes, it feels like my life is following a looping path, bringing me back to find the peace I've only felt in my earliest days.

Dave Griffin on Running

We are most true to ourselves when we're young. As children, we're transparent, uninhibited.

We are honest about how we feel. Love, joy, and sadness are expressed in the moment we notice them. Forgiveness is easy. Life is simple.

The emotion that changes everything is fear. Angry words, unfortunate events and misguided people crash into our lives, and we're never the same.

At first, we're simply unsettled by it, because being afraid feels so different in the innocence of our childhood. Then fear comes again, and we begin to make choices. Will we fight, or will we flee?

Flee, and life becomes a lengthy retreat.

When I first started, I didn't know that running would become a means of fighting back, but it did. I would go through an unsettled day, and then rid myself of the fear as I struggled through a workout. At times, it seemed like I was fighting the world. And when each workout ended, I felt a sense of release.

But fear is persistent. Things like confrontation, uncertainty and failure terrified me.

Racing became my battleground. Once, in my senior year of high school, I cursed out loud as I strained to chase down the leader. I don't know where the anger came from, but it made me tenacious on that particular day. I still finished second, but with a new understanding of my own capability. I could be strong even against unlikely odds.

There were races when my apprehension was the hardest opponent. Sometimes I crumbled in the face of it, but I always learned something from the struggle.

I learned that I can control my thinking and my actions, no matter what might be raging around me. I've crested the hills that make some people turn around, and then I kept running, leaving those hills behind me.

After being afraid and still moving forward so many times, I've found that nothing is as scary as I think it might be. My fear has been more restricting than any other foe.

Learning that changed my life.

Running taught me more. I learned that all success requires that same simple principles. Discipline, determination and work ethic will take you far, no matter what goals you're chasing. Accountability puts you in control of yourself and makes circumstance less impactful.

Running taught me that sustainability requires patience and contentment demands humility.

Now these lessons are rooted in my person, so much so that situational responses have become reflex. Life is getting easier.

Most of things from my childhood are gone, never to be recreated. For the longest time, that made me sad. But now I understand that what I loved about being a boy wasn't in things.

I loved waking up on an unplanned day, with nothing more than open space to fill the time. I loved finding a crayfish in the stream down the street, and chasing it into a jar so I could take a closer look.

I loved the freedom of running through my neighbors' yards.

Sometimes, it feels like my life is following a looping path, bringing me back to find the peace I've only felt in my earliest days. Back then, I found joy in nothing more than fresh air and green grass.

I'm beginning to feel that peace again on my isolated runs. I even feel it in the fatigue after I'm finished, but there's a hard truth to be understood.

Fear is real. Only through our struggle will it begin to disappear, allowing us to gain some clarity about this world and about ourselves. And, only then can we find whatever it is we're looking for.

And that, after all, is why we run.

Chapter 1:

What you most love

In the earliest years of your life you discovered what you most love. Maybe it's time to love those things again.

— Dave Griffin on Running

Innocence

We all remember the innocence of childhood.

Sometimes, we miss the comfort we found in the simplicity of our youngest days. We miss the pure, unconditional joy. And after we've grown into adults, it seems like the peace of our childhood is gone forever, but it doesn't have to be.

Follow me, and we can find it again, in the distance.

I was born on a Monday in March 1961.

A picture was taken when I arrived at my home in Woodlawn a few days later. My brother and sister looked at me with a concerned expression on their faces. Their tranquil lives had been invaded.

We moved to Eldersburg in 1964 to a house on Carroll Highlands Road. All of my earliest memories are there. It was my favorite place in the world for the next thirteen years.

We had a wide chimney, a perfect target for a tennis ball when thrown from a child who pretended to be a major league baseball player.

The strike-zone was several bricks wide, but that didn't really matter. Every pitch was hit back to me by an imagined batter, and I fielded all nine positions. If the ball bounced in front of me, I was the shortstop who caught it. I'd make a throw back against the chimney, and then I'd become the first baseman who would catch the ball just before the runner got to first base.

Such was my imagination.

When I go back to the house now, the yard seems small, swallowed by trees that were in their infancy when we lived there. But when I was growing up the lot was an immense playground.

There was a baseball field, which easily converted to become a football field. There was a driving range, a basketball hoop and sledding hills.

Sometimes, the property became a battlefield where armies would converge. The older kids were given higher ranks, and they would command their troops against an invisible enemy.

We were shot by the invaders on our own whim. When I was hit, I'd call for the medic who would run to my rescue and give me a piece of candy, the exact medicine I needed to rejoin the fight.

On the other side of the world, real wars were raging and the games we played made that terrifying reality more bearable.

But fear was a staple of my boyhood. I was afraid of the boys who concealed their own apprehension with aggression. I was afraid of the punishment that would come if I broke a rule.

The fear wasn't all bad; it refined my behavior. I tried my best to do what was right and stay out of trouble, but it wasn't always easy.

When I was in motion the fear and the stress dissolved. I was often in motion.

I remember racing against other kids in a driveway while we waited for the school bus to arrive. We ran during recess too, using the fields behind our school for short sprints. These are my earliest memories of playing with nothing more than two lines that begin and end a game.

I was fast, but never the fastest. Endurance was my best attribute.

I ran laps around our house with our Miniature Schnauzer, Pepper. He was happy to join me, oblivious to the competition raging in my peculiar mind. I'd out sprint him across an imaginary finish line and bask in the fictional glory.

When Frank Shorter won the gold medal in the 1972 Olympic marathon, I don't remember hearing about it, but I do remember watching him win the silver medal in 1976. Shorter's performances led to a flood of talent into the sport of distance running.

At the 1979 Maryland Marathon, 325 runners, 16% of the field, ran faster than three hours. By comparison, only 21 runners, less than 1%, broke three hours at the 2014 Baltimore Marathon.

The disparity between the two is a different topic, what's important is this; my love for sport and my love for running came together at the perfect time.

Ever since, I've given myself to running and it has given back to me. I've given my time and it offered freedom. I gave effort and running bestowed rewards.

Running led me to my greatest friends, including the dearest friend of all, my wife.

It gave values that became guidepost and principles that have led me to success in a career that has nothing to do with running.It helped me make peace with the things that I can't control because it gave me the strength to realize that I can always control myself.

When I was a child, I learned what I most love. Now, I'm a man who loves the same things.

We complicate life. In the process of growing up, we're fooled into thinking that more is better – more money, more toys, more accolades. It's not that those things can't be good, but I've never known any of them to bring lasting happiness.

In the earliest years of your life you discovered what you love. Maybe it's time to love those things again.

I grew up in Eldersburg, Maryland at a time when there were many pastures and no franchise restaurants. In the early years, cows grazed in the field behind my house.

Later on, the barbed wire that had once kept the cows confined simply stood between my yard and a field of corn. I climbed over that wire hundreds of times to look for a ball that had gone astray.

Every summer, baseball was the game of choice. Home plate and the pitcher's mound were hard dirt. Grass had long ago stopped trying to grow there, despite my father's many attempts.

I was the youngest and smallest of the group who played; most of the boys were friends with my older brother. Though I remember thinking I was a good ball player, I realize now that whatever team I was on had a disadvantage.

We played on summer evenings until we couldn't see the ball anymore. Then, when summer faded to fall we put the bats away and changed the game.

When no one else was around, I would play football alone. I'd hike the ball to myself and drop back to toss a pass into the air. It would fly just far enough for me to catch it, and then I would run until an imaginary foe tackled me. I know my mom must have wondered how I got grass stains playing alone, but she never asked.

Those were the years when I learned to play, to use my imagination and to dream about doing something special. And as I braved the older opponents and all the risks that come with dreaming, my mother was always there, waiting for me to need her.

She had the perfect lap, the perfect smile and the perfect way of showing me the one thing we all need to know - I was loved.

When I began running in high school, I discovered the pure sport that exists between the lines that start and end a race. Most times, my mom was there to watch, even though I had begun to pull away from her.

I don't know how to describe it exactly, but I remember feeling an instinctive need to rid myself of the emotional dependence. And, in perhaps the most heroic gesture a mom can ever make, she let me go.

In the years that followed, running deepened my personal identity. I grew stronger and more confident. Solitary runs gave me freedom. I formed values that I could believe in, values that still live today.

Now more than ever, I know her mother's love is eternal. She never stopped worrying about me or wanting me to be happy. And, whether I needed her or not, she has always been there.

Someday, many years from now, I'll finish a run just as dusk settles in the cool evening air. I'll close my eyes and hear the laughter of boys still playing in the yard, and then her voice, calling me inside.

We love beginnings. Things like births and new relationships give us hope for what might lie ahead. To a runner, starting lines do the same.

I remember my first starting line. I was in fifth grade, and there was a cross-country race at the school play day. I had been chosen by my teacher to run because I showed promise when our class practiced the events. "David is going to win that one," she told the class with certainty.

I remember standing behind the backstop where the race started. A classmate leaned over and said "go get-'em, Dave." I don't recall much of the race itself, except the sad feeling I got when I realized I wasn't going to win.

The next one I remember was about a year later, when the end of our driveway became a starting line. There was a disagreement between me and a friend of my brother. Somehow I thought I would be faster than this older boy, and I accepted the challenge of a race around the neighborhood. I lost.

Athleticism was the currency of my childhood. Up to that point, a starting line was a place of anticipated wealth, but I found only dearth at those finish lines.

You might say I didn't stand on a real starting line until I was a freshman in high school, when I ran the mile at a pre-season track meet. With two laps to go, I began to pass other runners. I came up to the guy who was then our school's fastest miler and he said "pace yourself" as I went by him.

I never saw him again and finished third behind two upperclassman from the other school. In a lifetime of moments most are lost, but I'll always remember shaking the hands of those two runners.

I would describe that moment as the beginning of a life-long pursuit. At first, I thought the thing I was pursuing was victory; I loved winning.

And so I sought out meaningful starting lines. I worked hard to prepare, and I stepped toward them anticipating glory. Sometimes I found it, sometimes I didn't, but my thirst was unquenchable.

Now I understand that I was pursuing more than shallow things. I was searching for the best of myself, and over time I came close to finding it.

We love beginnings for the hope they give us. We appreciate endings less.

When a relationship ends, we hurt. When a life ends, we mourn. And the longer we live, the more we leave behind. We will lose pets. Work will be completed. Aspirations will fade.

Most of my starting lines are behind me now; I know that. But running has taught me how to start and how to finish.

There are times when I wish I could run each race again. I could do better, or at least appreciate it more. Then I realize that regret has no place when you have loved a gift, and it has loved you back.

I remember the first running of the Main Street Mile in 1982, when the idea of a downhill mile created excitement for all the local runners. I entered hoping to win, but was only able to manage third place.

I came back in 1983 thinking I was better prepared for a fast mile. I only shaved two-tenths of a second off my time, finishing seventh. After that, I decided the race was too short for this distance runner.

When I finally returned to the event in 1995, it wasn't to race; it was to join the growing family tradition that's continued to this day. My daughter, Katie, was five years old then.

It was, of course, not her but me who wanted to run the mile together. But when she arrived and joined the gathering crowd, she became excited.

We settled ourselves near the back of the pack and waited for the start. Then we ran along in the cool evening air. After a short while she tired, stopped, walked over to a curb, and sat down. I sat beside her.

We chatted for a few minutes, and as I looked away, she sprang to her feet and began running again. I chased behind her, the giggling loud enough for everyone nearby to hear. She ran as long as the laughter continued before stopping again and finding another curbside.

In the years after adolescence begins, it can be hard to know what your children are thinking. We see their emotions, but sometimes don't know what's creating them. When they are younger, it's easier to figure things out.

The next time Katie jumped up and started running, I chased her again, pretending that she had surprised me.

She was thrilled to keep me guessing, continuing the routine until she could hear the noise from the finishing area. Then, she held my hand and we ran there.

My son, Paul, first ran the Main Street Mile in 1997. We have a picture from that day. His cheeks were blush red, like any five-year old boy's would be after playing in the cool evening air.

Mickey Mouse danced on the leg of his sweatpants, and his bright blue sweatshirt drew attention. His face was gleeful, showing he'd just done something wonderful, and in his hands he embraced his very first finishing medal from the Main Street Mile.

About thirty minutes earlier, I was with him as we waited for the start. He was excited, didn't feel the apprehension felt by the serious runners. The excitement made him antsy, as if we were waiting for Christmas morning to arrive.

When it was time to go to the starting line, he held my hand and bounced along. We settled ourselves near the back of the crowd. He wasn't concerned about appearances or competition; he was immersed in his own experience.

We ran side by side in the chilly air. His sneakers made a clapping sound on the pavement and his clothes swooshed with the movement. When his breathing got heavy, he slowed but never walked. The smile never left his face.

Near the end, he sprinted to the finish line, encourage by the cheering crowd. He looked back at me as if to say "follow me", and I did, until we stopped in the finishing shoot and celebrated together.

They handed him the medal and he started looking for his mom. When we found her, she took a picture of him with his rosy cheeks and me with my proud grin.

Children have an innate sense of living. They stay in the moment and appreciate what's in front of them. There is no worry, no threat of failure, just living.

My children taught me this - sometimes, just living is enough.

I was sitting on our couch, alone in the quiet living room, and I could hear him slowly creeping up the stairs. So I rushed behind the old chair in the corner and waited.

I looked with one eye, until I saw my brother cresting the stairs and searching the room for his enemy. Then he spied me and I jumped from my hiding place, knowing the battle was about to begin.

I'm sure I squealed with excitement as we circled one another, each looking for the first advantage, until one of us would lurch toward the other, and we would tumble onto the floor to roughhouse.

He made me feel big and strong, letting it be an even fight. Sometimes, he even let me win, sprawling out still on the floor that he could feel shake with my victory dance.

He could have ignored me, many older brothers do, but the four years that separated us were never an issue to him. We were friends.

We learned to play baseball like all kids did back then, with an improvised field and shoddy equipment. A broom handle would suffice for a bat and almost anything round could be a ball.

There were usually five of us, two of his friends and one of mine, and my brother would team-up with us little guys and make up for the disadvantage with his own ability.

He was good, making the all-star teams when he began playing organized ball. I watched, and developed a growing fondness for my very first hero.

He was comfortable with himself, confident, and willing to test his athletic ability against questionable odds. His intense competiveness was tempered with a calm demeanor, so he moved from rivalry to friendship with ease.

I tried to be like him, always playing center field when I had the chance, but life moved me in a different direction; I became a runner.

By then, he had begun the ironic passage that we all take, the rush away from the youthfulness we yearn for later. He wasn't around much when I was running in high school.

As hard as it was to compare our athletic pursuits, I wanted to match his accomplishments. It wasn't until my senior year, when I began to place in the championship races, that I felt my athletic success was worthy of his.

I can't really articulate why I felt the need to compare myself to him. All I know for sure is that the adoration hasn't faded; I still admire my brother.

When we're together, we don't talk about any of this; so much time has passed. We talk about what's happening now, we share our plans, and occasionally we wallow in the challenges that come with getting older.

Every worthy pursuit begins with a catalyst, something that moves us in the right direction. I don't want to write another word about running without acknowledging mine.

Chapter 2:

Our Fear

Our fear becomes our greatest constraint.

— Dave Griffin on Running

Fear

Fear comes in many forms – anxiety, doubt, uneasiness – and every one restricts you. Fear is a self-made emotion, a product of our apprehension.

If you want to do something, achieve something or become something, fear is the first obstacle you'll need to overcome.

Tuesdays with Morrie, written by Mitch Albom, is a book about life, as seen through the eyes of a wise man who's dying. Morrie, one of Albom's old college professors, had Lou Gehrig's disease. He was slowly but surely dying; his body was becoming a useless, curling bundle.

And yet, Morrie was more alive than anyone I've known personally. He embraced each day and relished his relationships. And, he wanted to teach the wisdom he'd taken from his life and through his illness. Mitch Albom became his student for one last class.

Tuesdays with Morrie has nothing to do with running. But I was looking for something meaningful to share with the members of my running program, Flying Feet, and I sometimes find those things in unlikely places.

My runners were about to run some important races. They had been preparing for months, and I knew they were ready physically. But sometimes that's the easy part. Having faith once the preparation is complete can be harder.

I'm not sure I can fully articulate why that's true. The reasons are too complex. Human experience is too diverse.

All I can say for sure is each person's challenges are unique. Some people lack confidence; they're plagued by the persistence of doubtful voices. Other people question their own worthiness, wondering if they deserve success.

And so, after months of preparation and with only a short time separating my runners from their big race, I wanted to share something to help them get passed all that.

Before one of our workouts, I stood in front of the group and read a few paragraphs that ended with one of Morrie's profound lessons; "Once you learn how to die, you learn how to live."

I gave them a moment to think about what I read, and I could see shaking heads and knowing smiles.

We try to ignore the things we fear, but they always lurk close by. We can see the dark shadows as we look over our own shoulder, and our fear becomes our greatest constraint.

We fear failure. We think it devalues us. We're concerned about what others might think, and so we cower, never recognizing the self-sabotage that precedes a failed attempt.

This is hard stuff. No one can work through it for you, it's an internal battle that's won or lost in private contemplation.

Runners are lucky. We have a circle of support. When one of us succeeds, others celebrate because we know what success requires. When one of us fails, others give support because we know how much it hurts.

The trick is to give yourself the same unconditional acceptance because, using Morrie's wisdom, once you learn how to fail, you learn how to succeed.

Death is a part of life just as failure is a part of success.

Ready yourself. Make peace. Only then can you fully immerse yourself in the pursuit of what you want from running and from life.

When I was a freshman in high school, I wasn't exactly comfortable in a crowd, particularly one that included older kids. So, riding a school bus filled with a rowdy track team wasn't my favorite thing to do.

Sitting in a parked bus was even worse, but that's what we were doing in the parking lot next to Westminster High School.

On the bus were the elders of South Carroll Track and Field, the upper-class superstars. My peers of the time will remember the names: Aleshire, Woodward, Llera, among others.

I was mildly intimated by these guys, not that they did anything to deserve that. Their confidence seemed unusual to me because it didn't exist in a freshman's world. We never talked about it; the four-year canyon between seniors and freshman is rarely crossed.

It was my first high-profile track meet, the Tri-State Conference Championships. We must have arrived early, because I remember sitting on the bus for a while, near my teammates who would join me to run the two-mile relay.

We would each run a half mile, two laps. Some say it's the most painful event in high school track, wedged somewhere between a sprint and distance race. By the time you finish the first lap, you're already in oxygen debt. Sometime during the second lap, the discomfort becomes agony. Only a runner's resolve can carry him to the finish, where he'll spend several minutes gasping and sometimes, in one of the less glamorous realities of the sport, retching.

Ours was the first event, so we'd need to get ready as soon as the team exited the bus.

If you never ran track, I should tell you that the four-person order in a relay is an important thing.

The first runner asserts a team's intention. A good position at the end of this leg is a statement of strength – "we're in this thing to win it."

Maintaining is the job of the second and third runners, and while moving up is celebrated, holding the team's place is their real job.

The final leg is the position of responsibility, the anchor as it's called. If the anchor receives the baton with a chance to place, he runs feeling the collective stares of his teammates, as their fates rise and fall with him.

Sitting on the bus, the four of us wondered what our order would be, so we asked our coach, and he answered loudly for the entire team to hear.

"Horigan," was the first name. I was relieved. On occasion, I had run the first leg, and I was happy to take a less glamorous role.

"Fyler," came next. I became anxious.

I waited to hear the next name, unprepared for what my coach was about to do. "Hogman," he said.

If you're lucky, from time to time, you get pushed into a situation that you don't think you're ready for. "Griffin," our coach finally said.

Over the course of a track season, you compete against the schools of your conference several times, so I was already familiar with the other team's runners. Our relay team couldn't match up against the best, so when the gun sounded I began to hope that we'd quickly fall out of contention. But as our third runner rushed towards me, he held the final scoring position. Team points and conference ribbons were at stake.

I stood on the track, next to the bigger, older and faster runner who would anchor the team just behind us. We glanced at one another, and then turned our attention to the guys sprinting our way.

I grabbed the baton and started running faster than I should have. If I was going to be caught, I didn't want it to be during the first lap.

My teammates lined the inside of the track as I came around and ran by them. Their shouts roused me from the fog I was about to enter, and I was gifted with a shot of pure adrenalin.

The backstretch is a lonely place on the final lap. The noise from the crowd on the other side was silenced under my own breathing.

When I reached the final turn, I still hadn't been passed, but I had no idea how much distance I had on the runner behind me. Looking back now, I'm sure the blind uncertainty terrified me, and it was fear more than fortitude that got me to the line where my teammates were waiting. All I remember from the moment they surrounded me was Fyler saying, "You didn't let him catch you, Dave!"

Later that night, I watched Chris Fox from Martinsburg High School run the two-mile. Rumor had it that Fox, who later became one of the best distance runners in the country, would try to break nine minutes. Moments after the gun sounded, he was already far ahead of the others, and I watched him run by me, lap after blazing 67.5-second lap.

In one night, I became aware of two important realities: I am capable of more than I think and human potential is beyond imagination.

Ever since, I've been trying to make those two realities one.

There was a circle of rust on the roof of my first car, an old, white Plymouth Valiant. The circle was the size of a glue bottle, one that had been left behind by my friend, Jim Kriete.

I found the bottle on a Saturday morning, along with coins that had been glued to the passenger side window. Apparently, Jim had been in a hurry when he made his mischief, because the sides of the bottle were covered with rivers of dried glue, and the rivers ran into a corrosive lake that surrounded the bottle.

You might think the rust circle would have upset me, but it seemed almost fitting. A Plymouth Valiant wasn't exactly a dream car for a sixteen-year-old boy. At least mine was branded.

Some of my earliest memories of Jim are from eighth grade. In the winter, our gym classes held wrestling tournaments, and the winners went on to wrestle the winners of other classes until a team champion was crowned. There were two eighth grade teams, and the team champions wrestled each other to determine who would become the school champ.

Whenever I think of it now, I can hear Jim cheering for me from the side of the mat as I wrestled. We had been friends for a while, but I don't remember appreciating his support until then.

Jim's encouragement helped me win the team championship, and I went on to wrestle for the school title, where the entire eighth grade watched me spend six minutes trying to avoid getting pinned.

Jim and I both joined the cross-country team for the first time when we were high school sophomores. After having some success on the track team as a freshman, cross-country seemed like the right fall sport for me. I can't tell you why Jim joined the team, but I was glad to have him there.

My memory doesn't hold many clear pictures from those days. I have fuzzy recollections of places and events. What I remember more distinctly are my feelings.

I was insecure. I was uncertain about myself, about girls and about how I was supposed to deal with all the frightening realities of life.

Jim was certain. He was a steadfast friend, someone who believed in me.

On the other hand, Jim was not a gifted runner. After races, he'd always feel sick from the effort, and as far as anyone knows, he still holds the South Carroll post-race barfing record.

I had a reasonably good sophomore cross-country season, but whenever Jim spoke to our friends about it, he made it sound like I already was among the elite. He gave me a good reputation to live up to.

I was quiet in high school, avoiding all the social occasions. Jim was the opposite. He was friends with everyone, including all the most popular kids. In those days, you could be popular for any number of reasons: athleticism, good looks, radical behavior. I wasn't popular.

Paul Martin was. He played on some of the more celebrated sports teams and had a tough guy reputation.

For some reason, Paul thought I was a great athlete. In pick-up games, he's often be a captain and he'd pick me first for his team.

Once, near graduation, we were playing softball on an elementary school field. I was in the outfield and Paul was the pitcher. I don't remember who was batting, but it was a heavy hitter, and I moved deep to defend against a long fly ball.

The ball was hit hard, long and far to my left. I went into a full sprint and managed to get to the right place, leap into the air and catch the ball just as it was sailing past me.

Over the sound of the rest of my teammates cheering, I heard Paul's voice say, "That's the best play this sorry field will ever see." I don't know if that turned out to be true, but I can still hear those words in Paul's voice.

At our thirty-fifth high school reunion there was a wall of pictures. The smiling faces reminded us of all the classmates who have passed on before us. Paul was one of the first to go.

I've had some good friends in my life, but none more devoted than Jim was while we were in school. I've had a lot of acquaintances too, but none more impactful than Paul. They were the first to help me believe that I could run fast and far.

Voices stay in our memory decades after words are spoken. The next time an old voice surfaces, decide whether or not the words are worthy of you. If they aren't, let them go.

But if the voice is affirming, repeat the words often and always remember this – someone believes in you.

I was fifteen years old, and I left my driveway to run up Carroll Highlands Road. Two doors up, I passed Scott Swartz's house.

Scott and I were both three years old when he walked down to my house and asked if I wanted to play. After that, we spent the next eleven years inseparable in our free time.

His mother died when he was five. I was too young to understand the pain he must have gone through, but he adopted my family, or we adopted him; I'm not sure which.

We did everything two boys can do together. We shared our toys, made up games and played sports in our back yards. We talked to each other without boundaries. He knew me better than anyone.

After I passed Scott's house, I ran the rest of the way up our road, and then turned left. In 1976, it was safe to run on the shoulder of Liberty Road.

I passed the gas station on the corner and the Drive-in Restaurant where Scott worked at night. I turned left at Ridge Road, and onto the property where the new Carrolltown Mall was under construction. I ran around to the back of the buildings and stopped.

I walked into what would become the movie theater, nothing more than an empty space with sloping floors, and I got down on the concrete to stretch.

There was a for-sale sign back in my front yard, and strangers were walking around deciding whether or not to become the new owners of the only home I had ever known. My parents asked if I could make myself scarce for a while.

Everything familiar was changing, and it felt like every perfect moment of my childhood was about to become a distant memory.

By then, Scott and I were immersed in the real world of high school. Gone was the fantasy, the made-up realities that used to fill our minds. Toys gathered dust.

I left the shell of the movie theater and looked around a little more, then I went back out to Ridge Road and continued my run. I ran passed the old farm with the pastures that bordered my back yard. The open space has since been gobbled up, but back then it surrounded me. For a while, I ran with nothing around me but grassy fields.

I've always felt deeply, which has been a blessing at times, and a curse at others. This was one of those cursed times.

If I had some sense of what came next, it might have been easier. If I could have seen how I would grow strong and fast, perhaps I would have felt better. But all I wanted to do was go back in time, bring Scott with me, and disappear into our imaginations.

I ran into the back end of Carroll Highlands, and then up towards my house. I slowed down before I got there, making sure our driveway was rid of strange cars, and then I ran home.

That summer, we moved away from my youth and to a house on Danmarth Road. It was a beautiful place, farther away from the urban sprawl, and over time I came to love it.

I can't say exactly when I found the courage to leave childhood behind. It was more of an evolution than an awakening. My runs got longer and my workouts harder. Friday night lights shined on cinders, and running was becoming a part of me.

As it did, my confidence grew. I spoke up more and stood up for what I thought was right. I started to become comfortable with myself. Once that happened, everything else became more comfortable too.

If you run, you know that things can change quickly. You can feel fantastic one moment, only to enter a period of drudgery the next. But the opposite is also true. You can feel constrained and heavy early in a run, and totally fluid and free later. That's just how it is.

Kids can't understand this, at least I couldn't. For a time, I thought I'd always be a child. And I thought my best friend would always live two doors down.

The real world eventually finds all of us, and it can be a harsh reality, until you realize that you're strong enough for anything.

If you've not found that strength yet, keep running.

We went through the first lap in seventy-two seconds, one quarter of a mile into the 1984 six-race Twilight Series. Chris Chattin and Jim Shank were leading. I was on their heels.

Back then, the Westminster Road Runners Club's Twilight Series began with a two-miler on the track and finished six weeks later with a ten-mile road race. In between the two, race distances gradually increased, with a cross-country race thrown in for good measure.

I didn't like racing on the track. The races were too short, and I preferred the road where I could cruise along in my comfort zone.

Jim, one of the runners I was chasing, was well aware of my preferences. He a track man, an elite sub-masters (35-39) miler at the time.

I'd get the best of Jim in road races, which is exactly why he loved getting me on the track.

The only reason I ran this particular two-mile race was because it was a part of the series. Otherwise, I would have happily done something else that night.

The week before, Jim had spent hours trying to shake my confidence. "There's no way you can beat me," he'd say. I'd banter back and talk boldly, but inside I had an unhealthy level of doubt.

We passed the mile in four-fifty, positioned exactly as we were after the first lap. Chris and Jim shared the lead. I was a step behind.

My position reflected my confidence. I was riding the courage of the other two, not once did I consider a move to the front.

The runners we were lapping began to move into the second lane, the race now longer for them. The running boom from the seventies had flooded the sport with a remarkable level of talent. That night, thirty-two runners would run twelve minutes or faster. Fifty-two, or seventy percent of the field, would break thirteen.

Our pace was even, so as Chris and Jim began to inch away, it wasn't because they were running faster. The inches multiplied, and by the time we reached the final lap, they had ten meters on me.

I didn't try to muster a reserve, to search for enough strength to find a finishing kick. My mind was already convinced I couldn't, and a body always believes what the mind tells it.

Chris and Jim battled to the finish, Chris winning in 9:43 and Jim two second behind him. I watched them and crossed the line nine seconds later.

After the race, a spectator came down to the track to talk to me. He said it was amazing to watch the three of us flying through the laps. Maybe I was the only person in the stadium who didn't think I raced well that night.

And the reality is my feelings had nothing to do with how fast I ran, it had everything to do with how I approached the race.

I should have challenged them, taken the lead to let them know that I had real intentions. A spirited charge may have changed my mindset, and it would have certainly changed theirs.

And even if I failed, even if I faded hard, I would have known that I had the courage to give it my best even when the race distance wasn't to my liking. That's something to be proud of.

But that may not be the worst of it.

My development as a runner was stifled by avoidance. I rarely raced distances shorter than five miles and almost never raced on the track. I know now that the lack of focus on speed was a detriment, a piece of the success equation that I chose to ignore.

Achievement always has a recipe. Leave out an ingredient and the result will usually be less than you hoped for.

I can't go back and re-run a race. All I can do is reflect and share those reflections with you. But trust me - it's better to race with fervor than with fear. It may or may not change the result, but it will definitely change the way you feel about it.

Chapter 3:

The Truth

It's important to face the truth about yourself. It's even more important to stare it square in the eyes as you race toward the finish line.

– Dave Griffin on Running

It's hard to describe the last six miles of a marathon to someone who's never run one before. I imagine it's much like asking a woman to describe childbirth to a man; unless you've experienced it for yourself, you really can't know what it's like.

The nine-year gap between my last marathon and the one I was running made my own memory foggy, until I crossed the twenty-mile marker and it all came flooding back. Doubt, apprehension, fear, joy, determination and courage all welled together to form an emotion not otherwise defined, and I realized the end of my race would hinge on whichever element would dominate from that point.

It wasn't just a race; there was more to it than that. In a sense, I was facing a defining moment. Not that whatever happened would change me, but it marked an important check point. How would running be defined for the rest of my running life?

There was a time not too many years before, when I thought I knew the answer to that question, and I didn't like it very much. A surgery in 2005 to "clean up" arthritis and scar tissue in my right knee was unsuccessful. I ran in pain for a while and finally gave it up entirely for over a year. When I started running again in 2007, I returned with the same gimpy stride I'd had before.

It took over two years of dedicated therapy before I was running without consistent pain. After that, there were many stops and starts as I tried to figure out my new limitations. Finally, in late 2010, I'd built enough strength and understanding to give real training a try.

It felt good to be running with a goal again. The weekly plan added purpose that made running through the cold winter worthwhile. Some runs went well. Others didn't, but I made it to race day feeling like I'd prepared as well as I was able.

The first twenty miles went as planned, steady and purposeful, and while I was still on pace to reach my goal, the gradual build-up of fatigue was getting hard to endure. And so, with just more than six miles to go, I was facing truth.

It was the kind of truth that many people spend their lives avoiding. It told me that my biggest dreams might not come true. It revealed that a part of me is cowardly and weak.

In the last few miles the exhaustion grew and my pace slowed, but my faith held just long enough for me to crest a final hill and see the last mile in front of me. Then I ran that mile faster than I thought I could.

It's important to face the truth about yourself. It's even more important stare it square in the eyes as you race toward the finish line. And that is what the last six miles of a marathon is like and how I'll define running in the miles that lay ahead.

Problems were bigger when I was young. Whether related to family, girls, school or something else, once a problem became entrenched in my life, I thought it was there to stay.

Time moved more slowly too, which may be why problems seemed to linger.

At the beginning of the summer of 1978, between my junior and senior year of high school, I couldn't have articulated what I was feeling; I just knew I was unsettled.

Fortunately, I had an endless summer to deal with it.

I spent much of that summer alone, running on deserted back roads on my way to Piney Run Park, were I ran deep into the isolated trails.

The well-worn pathways let me know that I wasn't the only one who found solitude under the ancient trees, but I never once crossed paths with another person.

Sometimes, I'd find a path that led to the edge of the lake, probably the secret spot of an adventurous fisherman. I'd run to the end of the path, and take a few minutes to look at the quiet water, appreciating the contrast between the simplicity of nature and the complexity of life.

There was something good about removing myself from the rest of the world. I felt at home in the middle of nowhere doing the one thing that always made me comfortable with myself.

I ran through pine forests, tramping on the needles that covered the hard ground. I passed grazing deer and flocks of birds. Everything was perfectly at home and seemingly at peace.

I covered the same route dozens of times, until the places became familiar, until I became a part of them.

Looking back now, I realize why I was struggling as that summer began. I was scared by the uncertainty of my future. The end of high school was only a year away, and I didn't know what came next.

I was also unsatisfied with my running accomplishments up to that point. I wanted to be among the best runners in the area, leave some kind of lasting legacy, but none of my performances met my expectations.

And time was running out.

As June became July, and then August, my troubles scattered themselves amongst the gravel of country roads and in the dirt of empty trails, and I became free.

I haven't been back to those trails in many years, but I'm sure they are much the same; they would welcome me back.

I felt more assured in my senior year. I ran with more purpose, raced with more courage, and even though my future was still uncertain, I felt ready to face it.

The past will always be sprinkled with regret, just as the future is unsure. But today is an unblemished gift, given to each of us on equal terms. How we use the gift, by and large, creates us.

❧

In the final miles of the first Bachman Valley Half Marathon, I caught up to Scott Douglas and we ran together to share the 1983 win. After coming back to win the race outright in '84 and '87, I came to the 1988 race with a feeling of confidence.

The course had hills in places where you didn't want them, but I knew those hills well. I had trained on the course hundreds of times with some of the same runners gathered at the starting line. Our sweat was sprinkled between the gravel of the roads. Looking back, the entire fall morning gave me a comfortable feeling of familiarity. Then the race started.

The early pack had quickly dwindled to two of us and I didn't know the man on my shoulder. When you are competitors in a race, you don't share much about yourself, so as he lingered a half a stride off my pace, I felt like he was trying to hide himself.

Wanting to get back into familiar territory, I surged just after the forth mile. I felt smooth as I ran under the trees of Beggs Road. The cool air on my face told me I was running well, and I passed the five mile mark realizing I had covered that mile in less than five minutes. It was one of the finest miles I had ever run in a race of that distance, but there was a problem. He was still there.

It was at that point in the race when my confidence crumbled. Suddenly I was running defensively and doubting my ability to keep up. I had to convince myself at each mile marker that I could stay with him until the next one. In the eleventh mile I lost the mental battle and he put a gap between us that held until the end of the race. In a time faster than any of my winning times, 1:12:24, I would finish second.

In a brief conversation afterwards, I learned that my competitor was Steven Clark. Clark had just finished a successful college running career but had never raced longer than 10,000 meters. He had spent the entire race questioning his ability to cover the half-marathon distance. It was only recently that I understood the irony in that.

It's funny how life teaches lessons in its own time. I guess that has less to do with what we're capable of understanding and more to do with what we're willing to accept. Either way, I find myself wondering how well I could have run that day if I had simply believed in myself for the entire 13.1 miles.

Each year, runners again run the hills of the Bachman Valley Half Marathon. On the course, lessons are taught but sometimes not understood until years later.

So, I'll keep reflecting on the races of my past. I'll keep remembering the victories and the disappointments. And, sometimes, new light will be shed on something that used to be unclear, and new hope will grow from the sweat that still stains the old gravel.

I finished one of the best runs I had had in a long time. It felt good to open up and run fast.

Whenever I have a run like that, my mind turns to competition. I start to think about my past success and dream about what might be possible if the injuries I've had in recent years would loosen their hold on me.

My son, Paul, started running in middle school, but he never had the competitive nature of his old man. He was always willing to accept whatever running has offered him.

I was still thinking about my encouraging run when I got the phone call. Paul was ill and on his way to the emergency room. Before I could come to terms with what was happening, we were in route to Johns Hopkins hospital where Paul could be better cared for.

The days that followed were filled with uncomfortable waiting as the doctors tried to figure out just what was making Paul sick. In those days, running hardly crossed my mind. It was only in the relief of learning that Paul was going to be fine that I packed a running bag one morning as I prepared to head down to the hospital.

That afternoon, Paul was asleep when I went outside to run a few miles. It was a different kind of run; I'm not use to city noise and endless concrete. I passed hundreds of people but didn't find one kindred running spirit, though I searched several times as I jogged in place waiting for traffic to pass.

I ran the city blocks around the hospital several times before I began to relax, and by the time the run was over I felt a peaceful calm that I desperately needed.

I wiped the sweat from my face as I walked back inside. I moved through the hallways and towards my son, thinking about how blessed I've been to have him in my life.

Things were hectic when he was young, but he had a way of reminding me to appreciate simply joy. I remember the belly laugh the lured me to play and the innocent wonder that led me to slow down and explore beside him.

It seems a bit ironic that he's taught me so much about life. After all, I thought I was supposed to be the teacher in the relationship. And, while I've tried to share whatever wisdom I have to offer, his lessons to me have been just as valuable, if not more so.

When I walked back into his hospital room, Paul was still sleeping. I stared for a few minutes and whispered a quiet thank you.

I know myself too well to think I'm ready to stop dreaming about running faster, but it's a dream that can't live forever. When I'm finally ready to let it go, I'll take an easy run and try to keep it all in perspective, and it will really help if Paul's there running beside me.

I stood in front of my Flying Feet group explaining the workout, even though most of them were already familiar with it.

The workout simulates race conditions, provides an excellent training stimulus, and helps runners practice the mental focus that is so critical to progress. It's no wonder they were apprehensive.

In fact, I learned some time ago that many of the runners I coach have a special name for this particular workout – the DDW, which is short for Dreaded Dave Workout.

When they were ready, I lined them up, and they began the first interval as I headed out to where I would meet them, 5,000 meters away from where they began.

Sometimes, after particularly meaningful runs, Deb Leathers, one of my runners, will send an email memorializing the day. The one she sent after this run was particularly poignant.

She began, "Mapmakers in medieval times had quite a task. Many times, they went along on lengthy and dangerous explorations and, if they survived, were expected to create a map of the new previously uncharted territory."

"When a mapmaker had drawn upon all of his new knowledge, he would create a map and then neatly letter across the void beyond: Here Be Dragons."

"Today's workout was the type that tells a tale," Deb said. "It can be a tale of hugging the mapped borderline safely, or of going a bit farther, to find out if dragons do exist in the uncharted territory. It is unforgiving in nature; there are no easy parts."

At this point, I was feeling a bit guilty. I coach people who run to enhance their lives, not to win championships.

Perhaps I had been asking too much of them.

Thankfully, Deb went on. "In our everyday lives, we tend not to cross into the void that has dragons. We stick with the familiar. We have meatloaf on Tuesday and spaghetti on Thursdays. We get up at six and read the news with our toast and coffee."

"But with running, we record what we have done like those ancient mapmakers. We log runs, times, weather and courses. We mark hills based on difficulty."

Then, Deb made her powerful point. "We run so we can step into the territory that we usually avoid. We can see if there are dragons, and if there are, slay them."

I watched everyone finish the workout, knowing I had pushed them beyond their comfort zone. For most, that's exactly what they needed, both to become better runners and to lead better lives.

Life can become routine, and that's fine, so long as you're happy with yourself. If not, there may be something outside your normal boundaries that you should finally face.

There will always be dragons. Some are too far away to hurt you. Let them be.

But others lurk nearby, and you have a choice to make about those – either let them confine you or go into the outlying territory, find your best courage, and kill them once and for all.

Just before the explosions near the finish line of the 2013 Boston Marathon, runners were living the final moments of a life-long dream. The elite had finished hours before; the runners still on the course had journeyed through more ordinary lives to get to this point.

Their stories, varied as they are, began with a compelling reason to start running. They employed all the disciplines a runner needs to improve, things like accountability, fortitude and patience.

They recognized potential in themselves, set a lofty goal, and worked hard for years so they could run a qualifying marathon; running Boston is an earned privilege.

They survived the registration process and made their travel plans as they began training to run on the most famous streets in running lore. They lined up at the start in Hopkinton, and were finally on their way.

They ran the early down-hill miles, captivated by the thrill of the world's greatest race, and felt the first signs of fatigue in the middle miles, wondering if they could make it to the finish.

They climbed the Newton Hills, saw the looming city, and gathered all their strength for the final miles.

Then, after having done so much to be worthy of enjoying the last few footsteps, the moment was stolen in a cowardly and heinous act.

Trying to rationalize what happened is wasted energy. You can't apply reason to something so unreasonable. The same is true of all the tragedies we hear about. Senselessness runs amuck, or so it seems.

But for a runner, something about this one was different; it happened in our sanctuary.

Running gives us peace. We find it in the solitude, in the alone time that let's us reflect and sort things out. We find it in the tranquility of quiet trails, where we feel a calmness that's missing in other places. Peace is in the exertion itself, because it lets us rid ourselves of unruly emotion.

And so, when the bombs blew up in Boston, the debris landed in a thousand other places.

But running also gives us courage. It leads us to exhaustion, only to prove that we can run through it. It gives us pain, feebleness and failure to prove we can endure.

We confront ourselves with the demands of running because, as we overcome them, we learn that we can also overcome the unthinkable calamities of life. It is the challenge that inspires us, gives us confidence and makes us strong.

We all tuned in to the limitless drone of news because it deserved our attention. But despite all the talk of mitigating efforts, we inherently know it can happen again. We will always be vulnerable to an unstable soul with an unjust cause, just as we are exposed to all the perils of life.

So we will keep running, in Boston and elsewhere, because it gives us the courage and the peace to bravely move on.

Chapter 4:

Venture forth

In the deepest reaches of each one of us is greatness, if we would only dare to *venture forth*.

– Dave Griffin on Running

Struggle

Struggle has a negative connotation. People, and even the society at large, go to great lengths to avoid it. That's a shame.

It is through struggle that we create ourselves. Embrace it as a part of life, because no amount of avoidance will take it from you.

And remember this – you are strong enough.

My parents keep a collage of old pictures displayed at their home. If I had to guess, I would say it was made in 1974.

The first thirteen years of my life are memorialized in that frame. There's a picture of my brother and sister looking at me curiously just after I was born, pictures of the three of us in our Easter clothes, and a few awkward school pictures, one in particular where my lips are pursed to hide missing teeth.

Almost all of my life's interests are displayed there too. There's a picture of me holding the biggest fish I caught as a boy, and another when I was reeling in a catfish on a family vacation. There's even a picture from when I received a Rotary Club writing award, though I doubt that my English teacher would have expected me to become a writer back then.

The one clear omission in the collage is running; I hadn't become a runner yet. That would happen a year or so later, when I went out for my high school track team.

Running was my springboard to independence. It gave me the confidence to stand on my own. I could compete with formidable opponents and sometimes even win.

The pursuit continued through my young adult years and by the time my most competitive running years were over, I had a foundation of strength to build my life upon.

Some of the pictures in the collage are of my sister and me.

She was my first guardian angel. On my first day of school she walked me to my classroom and led me to the door. After the teacher mistakenly told me I was in the wrong room, my sister returned to find me crying in the hallway, and asked the teacher to check her list again.

We shared each other's excitement when the holidays were approaching. I remember meeting her in the blackness of the living room on Christmas Eve night, both of us too apprehensive to sneak downstairs to see if Santa had come.

It's hard to describe the connection you have with someone who shares your earliest memories. I'm not sure I can. For now, let me just say that her gracious love was with me at the time when I most needed it.

Since our childhoods, I've been more fortunate, traversing this life without many hardships. Her burdens have been greater.

There are times when I wish I could give her the blessings I've gained from running, show her how I got the best of myself by risking the worst, and how I've found triumph only after struggle.

I'd like to gift her with the peace that comes by simply accepting where you are, and viewing the place as the starting line you've been waiting for.

When we were kids, the future seemed so unfettered, and it was, just as it is now.

I remember a world so large you could never travel it all, even in a hundred lifetimes. It lived in my child's mind, in the days when I would lay flat on the grass watching the clouds drift by.

I did that a lot when I was young, because time was as vast as the endless world, and I didn't feel the need to use it up so quickly.

I knew the residents of every house on my street, but not as well as I knew the nooks and crannies of their yards, where I bit into the rhubarb next door and looked for frogs in the steam several houses down.

When I was a little older, I ventured further away with my friend, Scott. We'd wake early and walk through the morning haze to fish at Liberty Lake. If we had seventy-five cents, we could walk to the end of our road where we would eat French fries in pools of ketchup at the snack counter in the grocery store.

I began running in this immense world when I was fourteen years old, escaping from my adolescent fears while I ran loops around the corn fields at South Carroll High School.

A school bus took me to far-off places, where I would race on the tracks and fields of other schools. Back then, diverse cultures could only be seen in the colors of the uniforms, and in the odd traditions of the other teams.

Once, we rolled into Damascus High School on the day they were playing their powder-puff football game. Grown boys dressed as cheerleaders pranced in front of our bus, and I was sure the people were as strange as the unfamiliar place.

Not long ago, when I was in the middle of a three-hundred mile drive, I bumped into a running friend at a rest stop. She was traveling to a different far-away town, and we somehow happened by the same place at the same time.

The world isn't as big as I used to think it was. You can get to the end of it by Googling in your living room, and when a cloud drifts by unnoticed, you can catch it driving the speed limit.

Now, it is the vastness in people I'm just beginning to understand.

I once saw a man with blistered feet early in a marathon find a way to finish, even though his feet were so raw by the end that a normal man couldn't bear to stand on them.

Another time, I watched an autistic runner, so limited that he couldn't hold a conversation, win a premier ultra-marathon, after being coached by my friend whose only incentive was rooted in compassion.

Traversing the human spirit is a personal thing; we each have to explore our own. I'm convinced that in the deepest reaches of each one of us is greatness, if we would only dare to venture forth.

Todd Ashley joined the indoor track team when he was a freshman and I was a sophomore, becoming the high school teammate who would have the largest influence on my running.

Todd was the first in a long string of elite runners who I had the pleasure of running with. He and I competed together against guys with names like Shultz, Sheely, Fox and Scuffins, all runners who would become national class athletes in the years after high school.

Not every high school runner takes running seriously. Many of our teammates spent a lot of time in the corn fields around the school, inventing throwing games that involved cobs and stalks.

Todd and I gave one another a measure of accountability. We trained together, doing the prescribed workout regardless of what everyone else was doing. The dedication gave us a feeling of mutual respect and a relationship that isn't fully defined by the word friend.

During the winter season we often ran inside the school, lap after lap around the first floor.

There was an exact method to running the hallways so that we didn't have to break stride on the turns. The runner on the inside surged in front, so as to place himself on the outside after the turn, while the other runner stayed wide and then moved sharply to the inside. Todd and I ran the turns with perfection, and a certain amount of pride.

In races, I usually watched him from behind, finding a way to beat him only twice over the three years we were teammates.

Running in his shadow wasn't always easy. I was too young to understand that I was becoming a better runner because of Todd. He set standards of performance that I would have never set for myself, and I became a formidable runner myself because I was chasing him.

In the fall of my junior year, Todd and I found out about a race that started in Boonsboro. It sounded fun, and his dad drove us there, dropped us off, and promised to pick us up at the finish - which was fifty miles away.

We were undertrained and unprepared for what we were about to do. While the other runners had crews to assist them, all we had was a few dollars to buy food at the stand that would be near the thirty mile mark. Fortunately, a crew helping Westminster runners recognized us and gave us some attention from time to time.

About half way through the race, I vividly remember lying on the ground together, neither of us wanting to run another step. I don't know how long we lay there before we found the strength to get back up and keep moving forward, but I do know I never would have finished the remaining miles if it wasn't for Todd.

Before my final season of outdoor track, my coach sat me down. We talked about how I wanted to finish and decided that my best event was the mile. For the entire season, I had the event to myself while Todd graciously focused on other distances.

The gift allowed me to win races in all our smaller meets, finish second behind Jeff Scuffins in the Tri-State Championships and finally win an individual county title.

Todd finished high school with personal best of 1:54 for the half-mile and 4:19 for the mile.

He went on to become a five-time national junior college champion and he still holds the NJCAA record at 1000 yards. Closer to home, he ran a stellar 3:54.6 at the Main Street Mile in Westminster, a course record that has stood now for twenty-seven years.

Accomplishment requires independence. You need to develop the virtues of success within yourself. But full potential is seldom reached alone.

So find someone who's willing to suffer beside you and able to show you that the challenge leads to something worthwhile, because it always does.

We huddled together, gesturing to the camera that we were number one. The cold, damp air didn't seem to bother us by this time. Elation has a way of warming you.

We had just won the Tri-State Track and Field Championships by a margin that caused the reporter to use the headline "Blow Out City." To say we were proud would be an understatement.

I have to wonder if I would recognize many of the faces if I saw them now. The thirty years that have passed since the picture was taken has changed us, I'm sure. I wonder too if the rest of them remember that night, one I'll never forget.

When we arrived on the bus, the cold, steady rain had put my teammates in a lazy mood. Most of them were wishing the meet would be canceled, when I stood up and voiced my anger. "Let the rest of the teams worry about the weather," I said. "Then, it will be to our advantage." As a senior, I didn't have many races left, and I had a lot yet to accomplish.

By the time I stood on the starting line of the mile that night, the rain had slowed to a drizzle. I was seeded third, behind two legendary runners. One, Kelly Long, had won the 4A cross country title the previous fall. The other, Jeff Scuffins, had dominated the track that season, and would later win the Marine Corp Marathon in the current course record time of 2:14:01.

The race went by in a muffled blur. I was aware only that I was on Scuffins' shoulder, running just off his pace. Each lap, the starter held up fingers to show how far we had yet to run. I paid little attention, trying only to hold on.

I don't remember much about the final lap, except that Scuffins began to pull away. I never once saw Long, who would finish third. I crossed the line between the two of them, propelling myself to a new status.

I've often wondered why I ran so well that night. Maybe I felt like I had to set the tone for my teammates. Maybe it was the urgency applied by my dwindling time in high school. Perhaps it was some combination of the two. All I know for sure is that I had never before been so focused. I didn't think at all. I just raced.

Too often, we all think too much. Between the day we are first told that we can accomplish anything we put our minds to, and the day we realize that isn't so, we become subject to the most severe of all limitations, self-doubt.

If that's true for you, let me ask you to use your imagination for just a moment. Imagine that you and I are teammates. Together, we're waiting on a bus, while a cold, hard rain beats loudly on the roof.

Imagine the bus is your confinement. Imagine the rain is your obstacle. Listen, as I tell you stop thinking about the weather, to let that be the concern of others.

Now, from wherever you might be, step off the bus, find your starting line, and just race.

I paced in front of the starting line knowing that I was about to run the most important race of my high school career. As I moved to the line, I looked at the runner in lane one, a reigning state champion. We settled onto the line, the gun fired and I was on his shoulder.

We were racing a mile, four laps around the track on a warm, windless day in May. By the time we hit the backstretch, we had already separated ourselves from the rest of the field.

The first lap ended with the starter holding three fingers into the air, but it didn't matter how far we had to go. I was focused on staying just off the lead. I don't remember much about the middle laps, except that I became aware that the entire stadium had stopped to watch. No one was throwing or jumping.

When we entered the final turn, I was still on his shoulder. By this time, he knew exactly what I planned to do, and he made his move earlier than I expected. He had pulled ahead by the time we came off the turn.

When I remember the final straight, I relive it in slow motion. I was wide open, straining to catch up. The roar as we passed in front of the crowd helped me maintain my sprint, and we were stride for stride with twenty yards to go. I felt it when he broke, and my momentum carried me across the line a half a stride ahead.

I lingered near the finish line congratulating my competitors, and then moved toward the infield where I had changed into my racing flats and left a t-shirt behind. As I moved in front of the crowded stands I heard a voice call out above the others, "Good job, Dave. Well done." It was the voice of my father.

The next day, there was a picture of me as I crossed that finish line. My arms were raised, and my mouth was wide open with a war-cry. When I got home from school to find the picture, my dad had left a note sitting beside it. The note read, "There's an old saying that one picture can speak a thousand words. This one does."

The note was a tangible sign that my dad understood and appreciated me. At the time, that's all I needed to know.

He tried hard to be a good dad, and he fought to control his natural tenancies of impatience and worry. It was hard for him, and when he was upset with me, I knew it.

I also knew he loved me unconditionally. When any one of us were struggling it seemed unbearable for him.

I finished high school with more uncertainty than I was comfortable with. I had no clear path. Not wanting to become a reason for my dad to worry, I moved out and began proving my independence.

I didn't know it at the time, but running would be my means of moving forward.

I kept my dad's note for a long time before somehow managing to lose it. Of all the things I've lost from my childhood, it's the one thing I'd most like to have back.

I was hurting, but no more than the other runners in the lead pack.

We had been climbing for nearly half a mile, about 200 meters from reaching the turnaround of a four mile race.

The course was merciless, mostly downhill for the first mile and uphill for the second, and then reversed on the way back. The pack was bunched around me, all holding on and needing the relief that would come at the turnaround.

It was my final race of 1984, and I was finishing a breakout year, running several races that were perhaps the best I've ever run. My running log still has a note on the inside cover showing the goals I started the year with: 32:15 for 10K and 54:00 for ten miles. I had met one and came within seconds of the other.

When I look at that running log today, I wonder how I managed the mileage and the workouts. I long to feel the fluid motion I remember, as one run reinforced the next.

I was hurting on that hill, but I knew I had less pure speed than some of the other runners in the lead pack. On the downhill, they might use it to pull away, so I did the very opposite of what my body wanted me to do.

I sprinted, using the rest of the climb to put distance between us, and by the time I turned around they were scattered behind me, still struggling to reach the crest. They all looked at me with desperate stares, and I knew the race was already mine.

The adrenalin high on the decent was magnificent. The pain was gone. All I felt was freedom, as my legs moved on instinct. Near the base of the hill, I heard the footsteps of another runner, and he caught me briefly, but he had labored too hard to catch up. He was gone as soon as we began to climb, and I raced alone for the rest of the glorious way.

I know many would say that I'm lucky to have had the opportunity to win races, and I have to agree. In another respect, though, winning that race wasn't a gift; it was a return on investment.

Great opportunity doesn't present itself often. Sometimes, when it does, it will pass by untouched or even unrecognized. It is only with preparation that we can grasp a fleeting chance, and turn it into something great.

Running is a proving ground, a place where limits are tested, and capabilities are discovered. Through running, principles are learned that can be applied on race day, but more importantly, in life.

That's true for each and every runner, regardless of ability, because speed is a relative thing, but moral fiber isn't.

Some say that life has defining moments, but I think that's a misnomer. We are defined by the decisions we make, the work ethic we employ, and the discipline we display in the years before the moment happens.

Chapter 5:

The comfort zone

We all have a comfort zone, a safe room we usually avoid leaving, afraid of what might happen if we do. With preparation, we can expand its walls, but even then, our greatest potential never resides there.

– Dave Griffin on Running

I remember a May race many years ago. It was a day when a lot of good things were coming together for me. I was beginning to understand how the specifics of my training translated into race results and I was applying what I knew in workouts. And, on this particular day with clear air and cool temperatures, I had chosen a race with just the right competition.

I was pulled through the first mile on the shoulder of a faster runner, and as we entered a downhill stretch we were flying. I felt smooth; the long, hard intervals on the track were paying off.

When things go perfectly in a race, there is little conscience thought. Thinking invites doubt and forces you take an inventory of pain. It's to be avoided. In its place is concentration, a firm focus on the task at hand. For me, in this race, my single focus was holding on, and it resulted in the fastest 5,000 meters I had ever run.

I should have been ecstatic. Celebration should have been in order, but there was a problem. I was running a 10,000 meter race.

In a lifetime, there are moments that change life's course, whether subtly or with significance. For me, this was one of those moments. I could have decided that a 5K PR was enough, and that jogging in the rest of the way was fine. I didn't do that.

The course turned onto a loop in a quiet park. There was no one there to watch us; it was only him and me, racing along the rolling road. I clung to his shoulder, refusing to let go and knowing, if I did, I would be left to watch him pull away.

I'm not sure I could describe the emotion I was feeling. It was almost like anger, but perhaps better described as intense determination.

We ran out of the park and began heading back towards the finish on the road we had come out on. Many runners had yet to enter the park, and they cheered as went past them, but their voices sounded far away, muffled by the concentration.

The last couple of miles were all out. I was just holding on, so as he surged near the finish, he pulled away to win by a few strides, but I finished just behind him with a huge personal best.

We all have a comfort zone, a safe room we usually avoid leaving, afraid of what might happen if we do. With preparation, we can expand its walls, but even then, our greatest potential never resides there.

That race taught me that my comfort zone is as much a confinement as it is a safe haven. Leaving it that day made me realize that I'm capable of more than I believed. And that simple understanding has stayed with me, giving me confidence whenever I've needed it, at least a thousand times since.

In Carroll County, Maryland, on a day so warm you'd like to be stooping in the shallow end of a back-yard pool, a tractor race will draw a crowd. I know because I was in such a crowd, searching for an empty place along the railing to get a clear view.

They weren't tractors really; they were riding lawn mowers with souped-up engines that made them fast.

An announcer made the affair seem formal, calling out the names and credentials of the drivers. One had finished third in an event that sounded prestigious.

There was a man with colored flags at the starting line. He waved one of them and the race was underway, but not for long. A tractor veered onto the infield, and the race was stopped to be restarted again, once the proper order could be reestablished.

I didn't count the laps, but after a heated contest, the driver of an old John Deer was declared the winner, and there were appropriate whoops and cheers from the crowd.

There were no crowds at the road race I watched later that same week.

The runners gathered at the start, just over a hundred of them. Within the group was an Olympic Trials Qualifier who was given no formal introduction. It was rather low key.

The race started, and the runners rushed off the line and onto a country road. In the distance I watched them go, moving over a rise and eventually out of view, and then I waited.

I didn't have to see to know what was happening. The leaders were getting a feel for one another and figuring out who was willing to go into the deep abyss that competition requires.

The rest of the runners were watching the leaders fade out of sight, only to be seen again upon their speedy return. Then, with runners moving in both directions on the out-and-back course, there was a chorus of encouraging words, muted to the rest of the absent world.

Racing is a private crusade, an internal battle won or lost in spirit only. Out of sight from everyone except one another, the runners warred with their own demons: doubt, insecurity, and fear.

I watched them when they returned, the first runner swallowing pavement with every stride. He was a gazelle, each foot sounding off with a powerful slap. His closest pursuer passed with equal grace but less swagger.

Then the older elites passed, the shadow of their prime visible in the powerful strides. They were focused, racing with passion and courage, just as they had in the years when they would have passed minutes earlier.

In small groups, and sometimes alone, the rest of the runners finished, joining a gathering abounding with mutual respect.

Some larger races have a gathering of spectators, and that's good. But, for the most part, cheering crowds are better left to the rock stars and the thrill seekers.

Real triumph is a solitary thing.

Single digit temperatures don't visit Maryland very often. When they do, it's an anomaly, usually one that passes quickly.

I don't know about you, but I don't remember hearing about the polar vortex before recently. It was one of those things that lay comfortably outside my realm of experience, and I would have liked it to stay that way.

But like so many other things in life, my personal preferences were never factored into the equation.

The cold by itself is uncomfortable, but the most deviant work of the polar vortex is its influence on anything that falls from the sky; once it lands, it immediately becomes a menace.

The slippery conditions caused me to cancel a number of Flying Feet runs, something I never like to do. I feel an obligation to the runners I coach, and canceling a run feels too much like reneging on a promise.

And yet, the safety of my runners overrides the hesitation, and our schedule has been impacted a couple of times.

A burst of cold was predicted to blast through on a Tuesday when Flying Feet was meeting for a workout. I knew it was coming, so just before sending my weekly email to the group, I checked the five-day forecast; the high temperature that Tuesday was projected to be eight degrees.

For a moment, I thought about moving the run to the next day, Wednesday, when the temperature was forecasted to be a more "comfortable" eighteen degrees. After contemplating for a moment, and considering there wasn't anything slippery falling from the sky that day, I decided I would stick with our original schedule.

When I sent the email, here's what I said, "This has probably been the most challenging winter since we began having Flying Feet winter runs. And while we are all probably wishing the weather conditions were better, doing that is like wishing life would be easier – it isn't going to happen."

"But here's the thing, facing the challenge head-on will teach you that it isn't as bad as you expected it to be. Go out, deal with the conditions, and finish feeling good about yourself. Then, when the next challenge comes along, you'll be better able to handle it without worry."

"With that in mind – it's going to be cold on Tuesday. Layer up."

I can't say anyone was happy about the cold, but runners came, and as they shivered and pranced awaiting my instructions, I told them that dealing with the cold takes, and builds, fortitude – I was proud of them.

When conditions are harder than expected, it's okay to adjust for time. But be careful if the time becomes extended because a challenge can easily turn in to an excuse.

If you want to do something, or become something, eventually you have to move forward in spite of whatever conditions are challenging you. The only other alternative is retreat, and when it comes to the things that really matter, that's not an alternative at all.

⸎

I passed the six mile mark and looked at my watch – 33:00. The last mile had passed in 5:07. I smiled.

In almost forty years, there have only been a handful of painless races. This was one of them.

I had surged through the sixth mile to shake the competition, and I was alone, floating, with four miles in front of me.

I had led races with a feeling of uncertainty, a tugging concern about what was happening behind me. But this was a race when there was no doubt about the ultimate result. I was certain about the laboring condition of those I'd left behind, and even more sure about my ability to hold the pace.

The freedom I felt is hard to describe. It was like a flowing amusement ride. The breeze was rushing. The ground sped by. I was doing what I loved to do and doing it better than anyone else who had gathered at the start.

When I first started running, my one-mile time was slower than the pace of this ten-mile race. I couldn't have dreamed about running that fast, couldn't even imagine the possibility.

Consistent training led to early success. Hard work always leads to good results.

It was a process. Once I broke 35:00 for 10K, I tried to break 34:00. After I broke 34:00, I knew I could run faster than 33:00. That's how it worked for me.

The frequent improvements didn't last forever. Eventually, I plateaued. That's when the real principles of success began to preside.

It took me a while to discover all the things I needed to do to get better, and to understand that hard work alone wasn't enough. The work had to be purposeful. To stay motivated, I needed to connect the work with specific goals.

Because I had a goal that motivated me, I finished that race with a ten-mile personal best by almost two minutes, and a life-long thrilling memory.

You probably already know the goal setting basics. Goals have to be measurable and achievable with a deadline. Omit any of these three, and you don't have a goal.

Measurement is easy in a runner's world. Distance and time are honest referees.

The abundance of races makes deadlines easy too. Pick an

event, register, and start the preparation.

Achievability is harder to define, and some runners mistake it to mean certainty.

Finishing a half marathon, for example, is an achievable goal for almost anyone, even someone who's never run before. With six to twelve months of dedicated training, you can cross the finish line.

And that's how many of the runners of today begin. In fact, though I've not seen a statistic, I'd bet the majority of people who've been running for eighteen months have earned the right to put the 13.1 sticker on the back of their car.

Many runners then go on to run a second half marathon and sometimes many more. Some go on to finish marathons. At that point, if the only goal continues to be reaching the finish, the achievability part of the goal equation becomes a certainty.

Is that bad? Maybe not, but when the challenge is missing motivation can stall. In order to stay engaged, it's better to dedicate yourself to something bigger.

In the years when I ran my best races, my goals became consistently more challenging. The probability of reaching the achievement grew smaller and smaller. Most often, failure was more likely than success.

I didn't know it at the time, but I was naturally learning what many great coaches are teaching today – if you want to reach your potential, you better get comfortable with failure.

This goes against all the jargon of today. We want immediate gratification, and lots of it. And the organizers of today's large races are happy to indulge us. Cross the finish line and you get a medal. Run the 5K the night before, for an extra fee, of course, and get another one.

I recommend, at least once in a while, that you test yourself. Pick a goal that's big enough to make failure more likely than success. Up the stakes and see how you respond.

If you take my advice, you'll need to train your mind as well as your body. You'll need to visualize success, because the body can't do what the mind won't allow.

Force yourself to think big. Imagine what you can achieve, even if there's just the smallest chance, and go for it.

If you fail, it's okay. It's not about attainment, it's about growth.

But if you succeed, you'll have a life-long thrilling memory, and you'll want another one.

1984 was a particularly good year, and I was expecting 1985 to be even better, but after a string of sub-par spring races, I was frustrated. My training wasn't any different, but the results were.

My target race that spring had been the Constellation 10K. It was an event I liked because most of the great runners of the area were there. The race began reasonably well, but I faded in the second half, finishing more than a minute slower than I had the year before.

I probably should have packed it in for the season. Looking back, it's clear that I needed a break, but instead I entered another race the following weekend.

It started at midnight, Saturday, June 1, 1985. The dark, muggy night surrounded the 300 runners gathered at the starting line. The air was thick and foggy.

I tucked into the lead pack in the first mile, just behind the police motorcycle that was leading the way. I was floating more easily than in all my other spring races and, before long, I was leading the pack through the second mile.

By the halfway point, I had pulled ahead. The motorcycle stayed far in front, and I pushed hard thinking that the darkness would let me hide from whoever was chasing.

Focus is the friend of a competitive runner. Thinking is to be avoided because it invites the enemy, doubt. That night, I kept my concentration and, just like in all my best races, the experience was dreamlike.

The second half of the course wound through a college campus, and I rushed past the empty buildings. The solitude was thrilling; I knew I would be alone for the rest of the race.

I cherished the final mile, listening to the muffled cheers from the sidewalk. One friend called out, "David, you look beautiful," a compliment I don't recall properly acknowledging until now. (Thanks, Rebecca.)

I took the last turn and ran another hundred yards to the finish line, and then turned around to wait for the next runner. The adrenaline high stayed with me while I jogged out to cheer for the other runners I knew.

I can't tell you why I ran so well that night. At the starting line, I had the same legs and lungs that I carried with me to all the other races that spring. There was nothing different about the week; my mileage, rest and routines were all the same.

Progress is simply stubborn. It hides until its own good time. That's why patience is such a critical element of achievement. Without it, it's easy to lose hope or, even worst, to give up.

Perhaps the most valuable running lesson I've learned is this one; outcome is an imperfect friend, but the disciplines of success are trustworthy. Stay true to the later, and the former will eventually show.

Dave Kovel was 100 meters from the finish line, running the final leg of a nine-leg relay race. His teammates, who had already finished, cheered enthusiastically for Dave to run faster. Andy Dodge was closing on him.

The race was handicapped at the start based on the projected finishing time for each team. The slowest team started, followed by an appropriate delay for the next team, and so forth, until all the teams were running. If everyone ran as expected, all the teams would finish at nearly the same time.

Each runner on the three-person teams would run three legs, alternating with teammates, around a one-mile looped course. Spectating was easy; the runners were almost always in view.

There was constant activity in the exchange area. Runners surged to finish their leg, tap hands with their teammate, and then begin to recover for their next turn.

The faster teams made up ground, and everyone tried to keep track of exactly where their team stood in the standings. I watched.

It was fascinating to see these adult runners, most of whom had never run track in high school or college, have their first "running team" experience. Until now, running had been purely personal, though sometimes bordering on social fun.

The first runners to finish their third leg cheered as the next teammate ran off, and before long all the teams were on the anchor leg. The excitement was at a peak.

Andy knew his team was doing well, but didn't realize he had a chance to win the race, until he heard his teammate's excited screams. The encouragement energized him, and he started to sprint.

Before the race, Dave's team had spoken about the importance of the final leg. He knew he was running for more than himself, so he responded with a kick of his own.

Thirteen teams had started with thirty-eight minutes separating the first and last. All the teams were now within moments of finishing, and the top two teams were in a dead heat.

It was the kind of moment everyone dreams about in childhood; a chance to carry a team to victory.

Dave and Andy live lives that are much like yours and mine. They work hard, they love their family, they carry the weight of all the ordinary troubles of life, but for these brief moments, they were simply runners.

As they sprinted, there was no thought of limitation. There wasn't time to reason about what might be impossible. There was only instinct, and passion. There was freedom.

It almost doesn't matter that Dave won by the narrowest margin. The finishing position was less valuable than the experience. Both teams embraced, amongst themselves and with others, sharing a moment they'll remember forever.

In a sprint to the finish, all self-imposed limitations are removed. Understand that, and perhaps you can shed those limitations for an entire race, or even for the rest of your life.

Chapter 6:

Find your strength

For the sake of your own well-being, challenge yourself. Find your own true strength.

– Dave Griffin on Running

I was in a lead pack of five about half way through one of the best races I ever ran. Even after so many years, I remember how glorious it felt.

At the time, I didn't appreciate it. I took my talent for granted, thinking it would last forever. Now I know how uniquely I was gifted; so few could even dream of having such an experience.

If I close my eyes, I can recall every detail. I was in the middle of the pack with two runners on either side of me, and we were in the critical stages of the race.

No one was thinking about pace. That had been established in the early miles. We were simply trying to maintain what we started, and feeding off the motion of one another.

There was no thought, only firm concentration. Sound, though detectable, was muffled. My racing radar was fully activated, searching for signals that would tell me how the other four were feeling.

The man on my right was struggling. His breathing was more labored than it had been before, and he was beginning to slowly drift back. Soon, he would fall behind, increasing the odds for the rest of us.

After he was gone, the runner on the far right tucked in closer, and the four of us passed the final mile marker.

After all the planning and the months of preparation, a chance is the best you can hope for. There are factors beyond your control – the competition, the conditions, how you slept the night before. Everything had come together perfectly to get where I was, one mile away from a dream.

The pain was sedated in the adrenaline, and I was still in a fluid rhythm. So, as we crested the last hill, I decided to surge to see who could stay with me.

When you finally take the lead, the only gauge at your disposal is the footfalls of those behind you. They were fading fast as I accelerated, and I just enjoyed the journey from there.

I wasn't very reflective when I was younger, just driven to win races. Looking back now, I know what I really needed is this – I needed to find the best in myself.

I don't think I was unique. Everyone wants to prove themselves worthy, if only to themselves. There are countless ways to do that, but all of those things require bravery and toil. You can't uncover your own potential without struggle.

And yet, there are so many contrary examples. The easy road is heavily traveled and we seem to build more on-ramps every day. Maybe that's why we live in a time that presents an abundance of both convenience and discontent.

For the sake of your own well-being, challenge yourself. Find your own true strength.

Once you do that, you'll know your innate capability, and you'll be able to use it in ways you can't yet imagine.

I stood at the top of an unfair hill, about half a mile from the finish of the Frederick Half Marathon.

Earlier in the morning, I had jogged to different points on the course to watch and cheer some runners I coach. Many of them had been training for months in hopes of achieving a goal; it was an important day.

I can tell with some accuracy how a race is going fairly early. It's in the person's demeanor, imbedded in expression. Good cheer doesn't always equate to good performance. A mood can turn foul when the discomfort comes.

But three runners in particular displayed quiet confidence and firm concentration, things I've come to recognize as signs of resolve.

I placed myself on the top of the hill because it presented the final challenge. Once on top, the finish line would come into view, and there is a gravity-like pull between a finish line and a runner who is about to do something special. If I could simply help them up the hill, the rest would take care of itself.

Just after I got into position, Sam Piazza passed. A track runner in high school, he started running again after a 30-year respite. He ran by me without even glancing to acknowledge my encouragement, and pushed the final half mile, finishing within seconds of his 1:50 goal.

After watching Sam, I began waiting for Vicki Borders and thinking about the discussion we had had moments before the start. "I'm having trouble thinking about running nine-minute miles," she told me. My response was quick; "Then don't think about it. Just do it."

At the time, I was afraid that I'd been too direct, but I learned later that it was exactly what she needed to hear. She ran the entire race without apprehension, and by the time she passed me it was clear that she would meet her goal. She ran 1:57:35, averaging 8:58 per mile.

Jo Anne O'Brien wasn't feeling very confident as the race approached; life was diverting her attention. When we met the week before the race, I told her to have faith, to use her raw emotions as a source of energy. When I saw her running up the hill, she was resolute. I could see the fatigue, but it wasn't stopping her. She pushed to the finish line, running 2:08:38, more than a minute under her goal.

These runners have more in common than the brave races they ran in Frederick. Each is over fifty years old with jobs and families that demand priority. Every day, their lives require them to face unfair hills on a course where the finish line is uncertain and there is no clear way to measure success.

That's why they set a measurable goal, so that they can come to believe in their own capability.

Almost everything is beyond your control, which is why it's so important to remember the one thing that always is – you.

The Constellation Classic was once the largest 10K race in the region. Held in the Memorial Day weekend heat and on a course that began with a three-mile climb up Calvert Street in Baltimore, it was also one of the most challenging.

The race was in its prime at the same time I was, during the 1980s, and I used it to gauge myself against the most elite runners in the area.

I have a picture of myself finishing in 1982. My form is deteriorating and my expression is strained, but I didn't keep the picture because I look good; I kept it because the runner behind me is Chris Chattin.

At the time, Chris was a rising star, and for a couple years, we had some close races. Then, he accelerated into the ranks of the elite, becoming one of the great Maryland runners of the time and ultimately running three sub-2:20 marathons.

In those years, I used visualization during my hardest workouts. I'd imagine that the best runners in the area were packed around me in the middle of a race. If I was feeling good, I'd see myself pull away in the final interval.

Many times, I was running on Chris' shoulder. He would try to pull away, but in my mind I was tenacious, always refusing to let go.

In 1988, six years after the Constellation 10K picture was taken, I decided to target the Metric Marathon in Columbia, Maryland. The race, which is still held today, has a unique distance, 26.2 kilometers or 16.2 miles.

I had run the race in 1987, finishing fourth in 1:34:43, about three minutes behind first place. My 1988 goal was to win, with a back-up goal of running faster than the '87 winning time.

When I arrived at the race, I was immediately glad that I'd set the back-up goal. Three elite runners showed up; and one of them was Chris. When the gun sounded, the other two elites sprinted to the lead, but Chis stayed beside me, and for the next sixteen miles my visualizations were in real time.

I don't recall learning why Chris wasn't at his best that day, but I didn't really care, and as we moved over the hills of Columbia, we passed through ten miles in 56:00 and fifteen miles in 1:24:30. By then, I'm pretty sure he was running as fast as he wanted to run that day.

He surged in the final mile, but I stayed close enough to run faster than my goal time, and see him take a satisfying peak over the shoulder.

Steven Covey's second habit is "Begin with the End in Mind." He tells us that all things are created twice. The "first creation" is our conception, a dream, and only after that can we move toward the "second creation," making it real.

And if you are willing to prepare yourself to achieve what you want, you have to believe you can, so much so that you can close your eyes and see it happening long before it does.

There's something about the middle of a run, after I've run away from the sluggishness and the stress of life has dissolved. It's then that clarity reaches my normally cluttered mind.

After so many years of running, I've spent countless hours in this state of meditation, immersed in my deepest intuition, and here's what I've learned: The solution to every challenge I face lies within myself.

I can be as strong as I need to be, as long as I believe in myself. There is no hill too steep, no bad stretch that can't be endured. I can find myself in the depths of exhaustion and still keep moving in my chosen direction.

Each stride is to be relished for its own value, knowing that it is a part of my forward motion, even when I'm not moving as fast as I'd like to be.

Running has taught me to embrace my own freedom, and to understand the responsibility that comes with it. I can run at my own pace, view the world through my own eyes, and suffer pain on my own terms, so long as I take ownership of my journey. I can relish the rewards as long as I accept the hardships.

In a hundred isolated places, on a thousand private runs, I've learned to accept myself, past mistakes and present limitations included. I've learned that pretense complicates and humility simplifies.

I must admit, I didn't always realize that I have been a student of this master teacher; the lessons have been patiently taught, allowing me to absorb the wisdom in my own time.

And sometimes running is more the facilitator than the teacher, working me through the walls of obstruction so that I can see more clearly.

There are a number of changes happening where I work, one of them being my own responsibilities. As I become oriented in my new role, I find myself thinking about the insights I've gained from my previous boss.

He is a seer, a man with great ideas. He applies his principles consistently, resisting the human urge to be drawn away from them.

There have been times when I've needed a lunchtime run to understand what he's asking of me, to think about his concepts and apply them to my charge. I return with more clarity and we collaborate to get the results we both want.

The other day, he announced that he's in the early stage of Parkinson's and that he'll be retiring soon so that he can focus on his own health and well-being. He did so graciously, and with a calming confidence. "The Company will be fine without me," he told us.

And we will, in part because of the lessons he's taught, lessons I'll be contemplating during many more lunch-time runs.

After he's gone, I don't know if we'll stay in touch, so just in case, I'll offer him these parting words: The solution to every challenge you face lies within yourself...

More than 2,000 runners gathered at the start of the 1989 Bay Bridge 10K. It was the tail end of my competitive racing years, and I had trained for many months preparing for this particular race.

I hadn't always been so purposeful with my training; I didn't understand the importance of it. I simply trained and raced without direction, and the results weren't all that bad. But I knew they could have been better.

Since my knee surgery in 1986, I understood the importance of resilience and patience. I began to align goals with deadlines, and I would map out training plans to follow. My results got better.

When the 10K race began, the front thinned out quickly, and I found myself in a pack of about twenty runners. The first mile was easy, as I simply moved with the group. I wasn't trying to run a specific time, my goal was to win, so I just wanted to stay in a good position.

By the time we passed the two-mile point, the pack numbered less than ten, and we began to accelerate on a long downhill portion of the course. We were clustered around a runner by the name of Jim Hage; everyone knew that he was the runner to beat.

It would have been easy for me to use his presence as an excuse, to decide beating him was impossible. I had never run close to his best times, but using excuses means you're leaving the outcome to chance. And, after so many years of racing, I finally accepted my own accountability.

There were only five of us at the four mile mark. By then, the weight of the effort was making it hard for me to keep up, so when Hage surged, I was helpless. Distance quickly separated the rest of us.

It's difficult to do your best when you know it isn't going to be good enough. I could tell you that my fourth-place finish was the best I could do that day, but that would be conjecture. All I know for sure is that I ran hard, perhaps harder than I'd ever run before.

It's important to be humble in defeat. The three runners who beat me that day ran better races than I did, and I have no problem admitting that. It's far harder to make humility a living virtue.

If you ask people what is takes to achieve, most will tell you something like hard work and determination. While that's true, lasting success also requires that you treat talent as a blessing and triumph like a momentary gift.

Then, when you can combine hard work with patience, and confidence with humility, you'll move yourself into a group that you'll be happy to run with.

Despite my airplane ticket, the hotel reservation, and my confirmed entry to the 116th running of the Boston Marathon, I didn't run it.

Only those closest to me can really understand how difficult that was. They know my story, how I've qualified throughout my running life, but always chose to take a pass. Now, I regret not running Boston years ago, so when I qualified this time, my friends shared my excitement.

I thought running Boston would be a simple celebration of my running life, a victory lap of my own personal design. But after I qualified this time, I wanted it to be something more, so I developed a training schedule and followed it closely. I was running longer and harder than I had for many years.

It's a mistake to think you know everything, even about yourself. Thirty-six years of running had taught me a lot, but apparently not enough to get me to a starting line in Hopkinton, Massachusetts.

The added training was more than my right knee could stand, and what began as a familiar ache continued to worsen even as I was running less. The MRI showed bruising and a stress fracture on my medial condyle, in the same area where I have arthritis from a much older injury.

The doctor who described the diagnosis understood what this race meant, so he was reluctant to tell me not to run. But after he described the risks, the choice was pretty easy. I want to run for as many years as I can, not risk it all on one final twenty-six mile race.

After six weeks of rest, I began running again, though gradually and cautiously at first. Just like I've done more times than I can remember, I started over with the oldest and least capable body I've ever run with. I can feel the slow creep of age, and I don't like it very much.

But there is a part of me that will always be young, where my dreams linger, my heart feels and my spirit lives. That part wants to run forever.

We waste too much energy on our physical self. We think it's our billboard, and we spend countless hours and dollars on the design and presentation. And even as we work to present ourselves to the world, we fail to see ourselves clearly. I know that's true of me, and I suspect it is of you as well.

So now, I try hard to let go of a racer's image, one that will slowly dissolve with or without my approval. As I do, I cling to this running spirit. I embrace it for the freedom and the joy it gives me. Sometimes, I even let my eager spirit test itself for its own sake.

And if I ever make it to the starting line in Hopkinton, I'll pass over it graciously, and run the Boston Marathon not for the runner I used to be, but for the man I'm still becoming.

My alarm went off at five o'clock, and Rascal Flatts woke me up. I turned off the noise and laid still in the groggy dark. It would have been easy to drift back into the peaceful nothingness.

My running clothes were where I had set them out the night before. I put them on and tied my shoes. The hardest part was already over.

I went through a routine of active isolated stretching, drank some water, and then walked outside into pitch blackness. The sky was moonless, which made the stars strikingly beautiful. I studied them for a few minutes before walking down my driveway.

Running in darkness has a different feel. The tiny light attached to my waistband did little to help me see, so my first few steps were cautious, until I was sure my feet knew where the ground was. The rest of my senses were hyper aware, compensating for my limited sight, so I became wide awake in the first few moments.

There's a feeling of adventure in the dark, knowing I'm moving unseen through the neighborhood. I could tell from the black windows that most everyone else was still sleeping and unaware that I was passing by.

I was grateful for the few porch lights that made a brief cut in the darkness. As I ran by them, a shadow would appear in the corner of my eye and sprint past me, finally disappearing into the grey distance.

After a while my run was much like the ones in broad daylight, because eventually I always move to an internal place. I become less aware of what's around me and more acutely aware of what's going on inside.

This is the time when I settle my own disputes and when I comfort my ailing emotions. I don't know why, but answers seem more obvious and problems less troublesome when I'm in motion.

Before turning to finish the last section of my run, I could see my house in the distance. I would have to loop around from the other direction before getting back to the driveway.

The upstairs lights were on; my wife was getting ready for work. The basement, where my son, Paul, was sleeping, was still dark.

Back home after being away for four years, Paul is a talented actor. I remember watching him in his first starring role, a high school production of Godspell. It was one of those enlightening moments when I came to understand him more deeply. He is passionate and expressive. He commands a stage, leading it to become the world surrounding his character.

But now, he's exactly where we all once were, at the beginning. He knows his dreams, can taste them like they're already a reality, but they aren't.

As hard as it will be, he needs to move into the darkness, take a first uncertain step, and trust what he can't see.

In the final moments of my run the world turned a lighter shade of grey. And when it was finished, I walked up my driveway, said goodbye to the fading stars, and went inside to get ready for the day.

Life is uncertain for all of us, but moving forward isn't a choice. The world will change and we will change with it, whether with or without purpose.

It's better to trust a blind step of our choosing than to unconsciously drift, because when the light finally rises above the horizon, we'll be in a better place.

Chapter 7:

Honored friends

Running removes pretense. Its demands can leave you vulnerable, which is why those who run beside you become honored friends, because they believe in your anyway.

– Dave Griffin on Running

Whenever I see Jim Bullock, my mind drifts back in time, and I am on some back road, joking with my friends. If you had been nearby, in some lonely house with a sleeping dog on the front porch, you would have heard us laughing as we ran past.

We were just getting started, some of us groggy from the sleep we were missing and stiff from our run the day before. We did our longest runs together, building a bond only another runner could understand.

When I think of it now, I'm amazed that life assembled such a swift group in a small town like ours, diverse, as we were, by occupation and age. I was the youngest, so I learned more from the others than vice versa.

Whatever the season, the Sunday sun rose beside us, shirtless in the summer and underdressed in the winter, until the pace began to quicken and we settled in for more serious work. We were quiet then, until someone gasped through a story to distract us from the sting of an unforgiving hill.

Jim was in his early forties, but he was doing the best racing of his life, running times that would win most of the local races today.

He had moved to Westminster from New Jersey in 1978 to teach Adapted PE for students with special needs. Soon afterwards, he met Frank Schaefer, and the two of them formed the core of a group that I would later join.

Jim, Frank and the rest of us did together what we could have never done alone. Those Sunday runs became a catalyst in own my development, a bridge between my running youth and my ultimate status as a sub-elite runner.

My mind took the reflective journey just recently, when I saw Jim at a local race. He had just turned seventy, and we spoke for a while about how well he's still running. Then I watched him, by far the oldest runner in the race, finish fourteenth in a field of thirty-four.

I asked Jim how he's been able to sustain his running success for so many years, and he told me things you might expect.

He doesn't run as often as he used to, or as far. He's added cross-training and some light lifting to his normal routine. He tries to eat well, doesn't over-race, and his workouts are kept at a level he knows he can withstand.

In a nutshell, Jim has adapted. He's moved past the days when we could run fast and far, and he's learned to accept the blessings in front of him.

Every day, every life, includes some combination of good and bad things. The secret is to embrace the ones that feed your heart, and release the ones that don't.

Still today, on quiet mornings, Jim and Frank run together. If you happen to be nearby, you may hear them laughing as they run past.

I have a photograph of Tanisha Fitts. She's running, just moments away from finishing her first marathon.

In the time before the picture was taken, I was waiting to see her approach. I knew she was struggling, but I also knew she wasn't alone.

Tanisha's training partners had been beside her from the time she first decided to run a marathon, surrounding her like mothers watching a toddler taking unsure steps across a wooden floor.

They helped her through long runs, speed workouts and many normal runs in all kinds of weather conditions. They encouraged her as she overcame aches and pains, something every marathoner deals with, and as she battled the fatigue of both running and life.

During the longest training runs, they divided the course and had friends join Tanisha for sections of the run. They did that with the marathon as well, so she was never running alone. At the twenty mile mark, six of them had gathered to carry her, figuratively speaking, from there to the finish line.

As I watched Tanisha struggle through the final moments of her race, the rest of the group looked at me with beaming smiles. We all realized something that Tanisha would only appreciate in the days that followed - this was a remarkable moment at the end of an equally remarkable journey.

I look at the photograph from time to time because it is the perfect illustration of the kind of relationships runners form. The effort of running removes pretense and builds mutual respect.

The runners in the picture didn't know one another until Flying Feet brought them together. They have various professions and different family lives. And yet they are like kin; their bond is strong because it was formed through honest effort and loyal support.

One of the runners in the group is Sandy Montgomery. Around the time that the picture was taken, she received devastating news; her father was critically ill. After several months of illness, he passed away.

Dealing with her father's sickness and his death was hard. Sandy had to face terrible realities, manage unbearable emotions and still see a blessing in the gift of a long goodbye.

Running became a brief escape, a time to place distance between herself and real life.

Sandy told me that she felt like her father was running his own race, over hard climbs and through bad stretches. All the while, she was beside him, helping him towards a final finish line.

And as she supported him, her running friends were beside her, sometimes one by one and other times in a hugging cluster.

Runners, as a group, are strong people. Because we overcome the challenges of our endeavor, we can more confidently face the challenges of life.

But we are made stronger by those who can see the harsh road ahead of us, and who run beside us nonetheless.

It started as a challenge between friends.

Art Webster was one of our training partners, but he was also an excellent cyclist. The rest of us were hard core runners and we didn't give Art much respect for his cycling. In fact, we teased him constantly.

Art competed in a 105 mile bike race each year that covered the back roads between Kent Island and Ocean City, Maryland, and our challenge to him was simple. Three of us, Jim Shank, Frank Schaefer and I, would cover the same 105 mile course by running it as a relay team. Since we didn't have wheels, we would begin running at midnight, five hours before the start of the bike race. Whoever got to Ocean City first would win bragging rights. Art accepted.

When the night of the challenge finally came, I remember standing in the midnight darkness as Art kept us honest about our starting time. Frank took the first leg, and Jim and I climbed into the van that would transport the two of us who weren't running at any given time.

I ran second, and I stood on the side of the road waiting for Frank to touch my hand. Then, I was running down an old back road in what seemed like the middle of nowhere. My heart raced as I watch the van pull away, the taillights disappearing behind a far-away turn, and I was alone.

I don't ever remember feeling more excitement on a run. I was moving fast, pushed forward by exhilaration. It was pitch-black, and I couldn't help wondering what was watching from the fields surrounding me.

We took turns through the night, and we had over fifty miles behind us by the time we knew Art was getting started.

The road slowly became more visible as the sun rose, but the air warmed quickly. By early morning, we were running in muggy, summer heat, and at a time when water was kept in a jug, not in little bottles, it was the beginning of the end when our water was suddenly lost. (It's a long story. Frank would be glad to give you the details.)

I can't remember exactly how far we had gone when it was my turn to run and I couldn't go. I took a stride and dehydration caused me to double over with cramps. After a short discussion, we decided we had to stop.

We waited for Art to ride by. He was struggling, but got a boost when he saw us. He earned those bragging rights, and I guess we deserved the ribbing that came with it.

We talked for a while about a rematch, but life took its turns, just like it always does, and there never was another challenge.

From time to time, I remember a day I wish I could live over again. Sometimes, it's because I'd like to bring back the pleasure of an experience. Other times, I'd just like another chance to do better. In this case, both apply.

Of course, going back in time is just wishful thinking. So, I'll have to settle for closing my eyes and remembering a long, dark, winding road where running tested my spirit, just like so many other times before and since.

In the early miles of the 2002 B & A Trail Marathon, I was trying to find the rhythm of the 6:50 pace I wanted to hold for the entire distance. I was three days away from my forty-first birthday, and I wondered if I still had a sub-three hour marathon in me.

The event features a full and half marathon. Both races start together, giving the marathon the feel of a larger race early on.

I settled in beside two sisters, Monica and Jeanne Grillo, who had their sights set on winning the half marathon.

Their goal pace was exactly the same as mine, and we began to get acquainted.

I hadn't run a marathon in seventeen years. My attempt to break 2:30 at the 1985 Marine Corp Marathon had been a disaster, so I swore off the distance for a while.

I never got back to the marathon by the time I became a dad in 1989, when my life's focus changed. I didn't run very much in the 1990s. Running was an afterthought, something I did from time to time without intention.

My first mile of 2001 was run with my children on January 1st. At the time, Katie was twelve and Paul was nine. After a loop around the neighborhood with them, I went off to run three more miles by myself. I memorialized the run in my training log with a note - "just starting."

I only ran twenty-four more times between then and April 21st, the date of my first 5K as a master (over 40). The race was a revelation – I wasn't young anymore.

I began training with greater diligence, and managed to break eighteen minutes for 5K before the year was over. Then, as the months began to turn cold, I knew I needed a goal to keep me running over the winter. A spring marathon seemed like a perfect idea.

I don't remember much about the Grillo sisters, except that they were perfect companions for the first thirteen miles. As we approached the half marathon finish, Monica surged ahead to win. Jeanne seemed content to let her, and we said a casual good-bye as she veered off towards the finish.

I went through half way exactly on pace and feeling relaxed, but in the space of a few hundred meters, I went from having great company to being completely alone.

My family was waiting just beyond the fifteen mile mark. They had formed a strategy to support me. Every five or six miles, I receive the twin gifts of their help and encouragement.

I reached Paul first, and he handed me an energy gel, which I consumed before reaching Katie, who held a bottle of Gatorade. TJ was waiting a few hundred meters beyond Katie, where she could pick up the gel wrapper and the bottle after I tossed them aside. Their smiles and cheers energized me.

But pain always comes in the marathon. It begins with a subtle stiffness, a telltale sign that the body uses to foretell the rush of discomfort that would be coming soon.

By the time I reached the twenty mile mark, the fluid miles were over, and it was only with firm concentration that I could hold my pace. I know my wife and kids could see the strain on my face as I passed them for the last time.

TJ shouted, "Tenth place and moving up" as I went by her. She roused my ambition, and I began to focus on the man in front of me. I passed him near mile twenty-two, and then found myself back in painful isolation.

My leg muscles became like guard dogs, growling as I tried to maintain my pace. The farther I ran, the more they showed their teeth, and I had to slow down. After that, all I could do was focus on one step at a time, but that was enough to cover the final miles and hold my place.

The Grillo sisters had waited to cheer me in, and I managed to smile as I went by them. Then I watched the clock click over to 3:06 just before I crossed the line.

The decade before that race went by in a blur of my children's milestones, but the competing priorities had taught me a valuable lesson – be where you are.

Life is a hard race. If you focus on whatever finish line you're chasing, it always seems far away. Live the mile you're in, and life becomes more manageable.

But life's more than a rush to some finish line. Whether you're running smoothly or struggling with every stride, something good is in this moment. Find it, because you only run each mile once.

Six in the morning was way too early for me to rise, but the alarm sounded and I knew Jim Shank was already on his way.

Jim was my training partner in the mid '80s. He was in his early 30s at the time; I was about ten years younger. We were both good runners who wanted to get better.

We met through the group who did their weekly long runs together on Sundays, though we knew of one another before then. Jim coached cross-country and track at Westminster High School, while I ran for rival South Carroll. I have a picture of myself finishing a high school race with Jim standing in the background. It was taken long before we had spoken a word to one another.

On one of the Sunday runs, Jim listened as I expressed concern about my job. I didn't like what I was doing, and

Jim offered me a chance to work for him at his running store, which at the time was the hub of the local running community. I thankfully accepted his offer.

We started running together on the streets around town and doing workouts at local tracks. At some point, to get our mileage higher, Jim suggested a run before dawn so we could get a second run in later in the day, which is why my alarm was set for six.

I slowly got dressed and put my running shoes on, then went outside to wait on my front step.

I heard him before I saw him in the dark, one foot striking the ground after the other. A moment later a shadowy runner appeared in the distance, and I walked down my driveway to meet him.

We communicated with grunts, each knowing exactly what the other meant, before the words began to flow.

The route we ran looped back to his house where he dropped off, then I finished the run alone. By then I was wide awake, and I enjoyed the adventure of running through the dim streets, knowing I'd still be in bed if it wasn't for Jim.

I worked at Jim's store for almost three years, and then moved on. Jim and I ran together less after that, and we hardly see one another now.

But I saw him recently and immediately remembered why I like him so much. He joked about a time he had outsprinted me to win a race, and I bantered back a time or two. We each helped the other discover something better in ourselves while finding humor in the process.

We ran countless miles beside each other, and encouraged one another even when our goals were overly ambitious.

How do you place a value on things like that? How do you express appreciation? Maybe you can't, but at least I can acknowledge it here.

Running removes pretense. Its demands can leave your vulnerable, which is why those who run beside you become honored friends, because they believe in you anyway.

Chapter 8:

The calling

We are all being called to become our greatest self. Listen to the calling.

– Dave Griffin on Running

Clarity

Look back at your life. Think about the struggle you've endured. What have you learned?

In time, we can grow wise if we only accept the lessons we learned through all our struggle. Meditate. Reflect. Your life has meaning. Find it.

Time passed methodically in the 1980s. Years were eternities, made up of deliberate seconds sounding off from a mantle clock.

My memories of those years are a series of snapshots and short video clips. I was running in the lead pack of a cross-country race at Western Maryland College. Local runners had been invited to join this particular race, and since I never ran collegiately, it was an exciting chance for me to experience college racing.

A runner just in front of me asked his teammate who I was and the teammate replied, "Don't worry, he'll fade soon." I can't remember anything else about that race, except rounding the final turn in first place, the two of them well behind me.

I have snippets of memories from all my greatest races. I remember when Rosa Mota of Portugal ran beside me in the final mile of the 1984 Cherry Blossom ten mile, the year she won Olympic bronze in Los Angeles, and four years before she won Olympic gold in Seoul.

I remember a few moments from my first half marathon, the inaugural Bachman Valley race. Scott Douglas, now a senior editor for Running Times Magazine, had run out to an early lead. I can picture Scott turning onto Lemmon Road as I was chasing him. With just over a mile to go, I caught him on Sullivan Road, and we ran to the finish together to memorialize ourselves in the race's long history.

I remember running half-mile repeats after nightfall at the college track, jogging to a beam of light to check my time, and then pressing in the silent dark to run the next repeat faster.

My daughter was born at 8:49 a.m. on November 19, 1989. As far as I can tell, that's the moment time began to move more quickly.

There isn't a word that describes how I felt about her. Infatuated is too juvenile. Obsessed is too harsh. My heart was simply taken, immersed in the life of my baby girl.

No two days were the same; she changed constantly. Her look, her sounds, and her movements evolved through a rapid parade of days that became months, which became years.

Once time started moving more quickly, it never stopped, and somehow twenty-five years have passed like water moving down Big Pipe Creek.

I ran a set of half-mile repeats on the track the other day. It felt much like it used to feel, relaxed early on and then harder as the workout progressed. It was almost like I was in my twenties again, until I checked the numbers on my watch. Am I that much slower, or is time really moving faster now?

I sometimes wonder how I was able to run as fast as I used to run, and I can't help but compare my present and past performances. I become frustrated at first, but then I stop myself. That's not the message here.

The illusion was in the past, when I thought time was limitless and opportunity lasted forever. The reality is now, this moment, speeding by as it is.

We have this day, that's all. Before it's over, immerse your heart in the people you love and free your spirit in the things you do.

It's hard for an aging distance runner like me to see time as a friend. I sometimes regard it as a thief, a silent burglar that stole something I can't seem to stop looking for.

That's exactly how I felt recently when I had a reason to look over the race results in my running logs from the 1980s.

I made a chart and listed every race, showing the date, event, distance, time and finishing position. Back then, I was running about twenty races a year and winning many of them. In dozens of races, I bettered my previous fastest time for the distance.

And yet, I never stopped wanting to get better, and I never stopped hoping to beat runners who usually beat me.

Just like every life-long runner, there's a burning ember deep inside me. By its purest definition it is a reason, a purpose fulfilled only by running and racing. For me, at the time, the ember was a competitive spark.

I developed a stress fracture on my right tibia in the fall of 1989, and I was forced to stop running for a while. Before

I could start again, I became a father and found myself with greater job responsibilities. My life's focus had shifted and my serious racing days were over.

The passing of years can blur a memory. Looking back now, I'm not certain why I stopped serious training and racing. It may have been the new obligations, or it may have been something else.

Maybe it was an unconscious choice. The burning ember was impossible to satisfy. My results never lived up to my dreams and I was beginning to doubt whether they ever would. Maybe, I just wanted to avoid disappointment.

You never know if a choice you made years ago was a mistake or not. Life's course is a fickle thing. Once we choose a path it's impossible to know where a different path might have led, and time spent searching for an answer is futile.

Time really is a thief, but it's also a teacher, and I finally understand that every moment is about more than the moment itself. Everything we do, or decide not to do, has an impact. We are all on a journey to become what we were meant to be, and the only way we can get there is to forgive ourselves for the mistakes of the past.

Fortunately for me, a new ember burns now.

It feeds on the movement that feels so familiar. It thrives in the solitude of quiet trails. Each run takes me away from whatever noise I want to escape and rejuvenates my spirit.

The old ember is still there. I feel it every day. I don't view it with regret anymore. I view it with gratitude, knowing it has led me where I never could have gone without it.

Just before the start of the Women's Invitational Mile at the 2015 Music City Distance Carnival, Sonja Friend-Uhl's mind wasn't where she wanted it to be. It was immersed in the heavy load of life, just like most forty-four year old moms.

The race didn't start until ten at night, Sonja's bedtime. And, the late start had done nothing to cool the angry June Nashville air.

All around her, some of the most talented open and collegiate middle distance runners in the country were warming up, seemly far more prepared for the race than Sonja was.

Sonja ran her first race as a seven-year old, a 50-meter dash. A couple years later, someone talked her into running a 400-meter race, a distance that seemed too far at the time.

She would run with her dad from time to time and her parents drove her to club meets around the state of Washington. It wasn't the early success that captured her interest as much as the emotional release running gave her.

"I don't remember making a conscious thought to choose running," Sonja shared. "In many ways, running chose me."

When she was twelve, her family moved to Lewes, Delaware, to be closer to the family that was scattered in the area. Sonja ran for Cape Henlopen High School, becoming a state 800 meter champion before moving on to run for William and Mary College.

During her warm-up for the Music City Mile, Sonja didn't feel the usual fire, and positive self-talk didn't seem to help her. As she approached the line with the rest of the field, all she could do was empty her mind and rid herself of the apprehension.

The gun fired.

The first lap disappeared, which is normal for an elite runner. It just melts into the place where lost time goes, and without feeling anything Sonja ran at the back of the pack, passing the 400 meter split in 71 seconds.

Her awareness resurfaced on the first turn of the second lap. She focused on staying relaxed and letting the pack pull her along. She hit 800 meters in 2:23.

When she had visualized the race earlier, she knew the third lap would be important, and she promised herself that she would race it hard no matter how she felt.

After college, Sonja became a fitness professional and coach, a career that worked well as she continued to pursue her own running. She's always felt that running was a gift, and she wanted to share the blessing.

Through the years, running taught her the value of perseverance, discipline, humility and confidence, traits she's used to set an example for her daughters. "I want to help them see that our bodies are meant to be worked, and that this also strengthens and opens our minds," she told me.

Sonja felt good on the backstretch of the third lap, passing several runners there. Coming into the bell lap she still had strength in her legs, and her excitement surged as she realized she had run the third lap in 69 seconds.

Every muscle fiber, every conscious and subconscious part of her mind was focused on a single task – run hard. She built speed coming into the final turn and she continued to accelerate coming off it. She was all-out in the final straight, passing two more runners before crossing the line.

Sonja finished sixth, but the place didn't matter. She just loves finding the best in herself, which is all she's ever wanted to do. That night, her best was a 4:45.68 mile, a new American record for women over forty.

My wife and I just returned from another vacation in Lewes, DE. I love running while I'm there. The trails are long and soft. The salty air is fresh.

On one of my runs this time, I stopped by Cape Henlopen High School to find water. A women at the stadium was kind enough to give me a bottle, and I asked her if she knew Sonja. The question attracted the attention of a few others, and for several moments they all talked about her as if she were a dear friend. The affection didn't surprise me.

A lot of people have talent. Few cultivate it. Fewer still, like Sonja, use it as a means to enhance the lives of other people.

As I finished my run that day, I realized I have a new reason to love running in Lewes, because it reminds me of one of the most enduring running legacies of our time.

Thirty-six years after running her first race, Sonja ran one of her greatest. The outcome wasn't decided at the time of opportunity, it was written in the decades of disciplined life that preceded it.

We are all being called to become our greatest self. Listen to the calling.

I remember the smell of corn stalks most of all, a sweet, leafy scent that mixed nicely with the dusty dirt under my feet.

The corn, bordered on the other side with a stretch of tall weeds, created a tunnel with a blue sky ceiling. I was running through the tunnel, alone, with my teammates chasing me.

It was 1976, I was a high school sophomore in my first year of cross-county, and I had yet to run a race. We were running a time trial, and I was having fun.

It was one of those hard runs when the pain never came, a rare thing I've since come to learn. I knew I was running fast. The blurry edges of my vision showed me a passing rush of green.

I rounded a turn, and ran down a hill that led me to the edge of a forest. Then I looped around to the other side of the trees and into an open field where the soccer team was practicing.

I raced down toward the track where my coach waited with a stopwatch; he wasn't expecting me so soon.

He stared at the watch and told me I was going to be the next Chris Fox. I regret to say my coach's prophecy never came true.

I did win my first cross-country race, a dual meet at Francis Scott Key High School. At that point, I was far from a race tactician, and I went out too fast, holding on just long enough to fight off the surge of an FSK senior.

It could be argued that this was the peak of my racing life. I was unbeaten in a distance race. My dreams were unbridled. Anything was possible, or at least it seemed that way.

I don't remember anything about my next race, or the rest of the races from that season, but I can tell you that I didn't win them. There never was a second high school cross-country victory for me.

I've often wondered why I didn't live up to my promising start in cross-country. Looking back now, I think the early success came with things I wasn't ready for. People I hardly knew began to expect more of me. I began to put pressure on myself, afraid I couldn't live up to the expectations.

Maybe it was easier to be disappointed in myself than to risk disappointing everyone else.

After my senior cross-country season, I took a short break, and something was different when I returned to the indoor track team. I finished my senior year more focused on what I really wanted to achieve, stopped worrying about what people might think if I failed, and finally started winning races.

Only a few people will understand your deepest challenges. Other people may judge you, and even question your motives. Let them. They face challenges too.

Lessons are taught throughout our life but not learned until we are ready to accept them.

I was running on an old, country road and passed a field of tall corn. The sweet, leafy scent helped me remember – I love running because it lets me feel free.

Free from worry. Free of constraint. Free to succeed or fail on my own terms.

We had just had a record breaking snow storm. Back in my competitive days, I would have found a way to run in a storm like that. I'm not sure whether it was a durable body or a reckless spirit that compelled me to do so, but I lacked both of those things, so my only workout that day came in the form of heavy snow and a shovel.

When I was done, I stood on the back patio for a few moments admiring the scene. The snow was beautiful. There was peace in the muffled silence, until I realized something was missing. There were no boot prints or sledding paths in the snow. My children had moved on.

It's funny how our day-to-day routines shelter us from a life that's constantly changing, until something stops us for a moment so we can take an inventory. It's not like I didn't realize that they were getting older, but something in that moment made the fact more real.

I knew when they were born that my role as a father would be the most important of my life. And yet, there didn't seem to be any instructions to follow, so I've pretty much learned along the way. Making it even more difficult, there are no real ways to measure success.

Both of my children have grown to become good people, and some would use that as a barometer, but they, not I, deserve the credit for that. Over the years, I've found that what I say to them has only a marginal effect. It has been their experiences, and their reactions to those experiences, that have largely shaped them.

What I've finally come to realize is that my highest purpose as a father can be describe in rather simple terms - to set an example for my children to follow. Here is where running enters the story, and where I have the opportunity to share something of value with you.

If you want your children to be strong, demonstrate strength. If you want them to be successful, illustrate the qualities that success requires. If you want them to be happy, show them that there is more to life than deadlines and responsibilities.

Running has allowed me to do all those things. As I've trained, overcome challenges and crossed finish lines, my children have watched me. As I've found joy and passion on my runs, they have noticed. In the process, they've learned more than they have from all the speeches, rules and punishments combined. It's not that those other things don't have an important place, but you can't guide your children with them if your own personal principles are misguided.

We all have a vision of what we'd like to become – a great athlete, a good parent, or simply a good person. Whatever your vision might be, the principles of running – things like discipline, resilience and consistency – will serve you well. And, if you should ever need a little extra motivation to practice these, let it come from the eyes that are watching and following your lead.

Chapter 9

In your heart

It is in the quiet, in the seclusion of your heart, that you discover what's important.

– Dave Griffin on Running

Scott Absher ran eight miles on Saturday, October 12, 2013. He doesn't need to look back at his running log to remember.

It was a cool and overcast fall morning, and as he left his house he knew exactly what this run was for.

His mother, Barkley Absher, was dying.

Barkley was diagnosed with pancreatic cancer that March. A doctor at Duke University Hospital, near her home, told her to focus on the quality of the life she had left. He offered no hope.

But hope was all the family wanted, so Scott took his mom to Johns Hopkins and to a doctor who said they had a chance. After that appointment, they had a celebratory lunch.

Barkley moved in with Scott's family, but refused to let her illness become burdensome to anyone other than herself. She joined the family routines and pitched in any way she could.

She became even closer to Scott's kids. Before her diagnosis, they would call her on the phone every Sunday evening. They talked about their lives like they couldn't talk to anyone else, honestly and without judgment.

As summer faded to fall the treatments weren't working as expected. Then, on September 30th Barkley was given just three months to live. After that, her condition seemed to decline by the day.

She was a giver. Family, friends and strangers were all her benefactors. She wouldn't allow herself to be the one in need, so Scott knew she wouldn't linger long.

"Running can help you sort through things so you know what to say," Scott told me.

The eight miles were filled with prayer and reflection.

The miles passed as Scott ran on the familiar streets around his home. If it began to drizzle, he didn't feel it. If a bird called out, he didn't hear. He was captured by introspection, examining himself and her influence on him.

She had always been his biggest fan. She just loved him, right or wrong, deserving or not, her affection was unconditional. He thought about how lucky he was to have such devotion in his life, to be held up even in his weakest hours by the strength of her love.

When the run was over, he had the words and the composure to say them.

"I thought I had more time with you," Scott began.

"Don't we always," she replied.

Thoughts and emotions flowed between them. He told her that he was proud of her, how she lived and how she had fought. He told her that if a life could be measured by the impact a person has had on others, then her life was immeasurable.

Five days later, after saying goodbye to everyone she loved and one day before her seventy-third birthday, she graciously passed on.

Scott and I ran together almost a full year later, and he shared this story with me. It reminded me of my own mom, always giving, always reluctant to take.

Scott and I have other things in common too. We've both found success in the same industry. We've grown our own loving families. We've both lived blessed lives, and we have to wonder how much of all of this is attributable to the grace of our faithful mothers.

In the rush of life, gratitude is usually unexpressed. Thank goodness that in the movement of a run, life slows down.

It is in the quiet, in the seclusion of our own heart, that we discover what's important. Once we do that, we can begin to build our life around those things, and give thanks to the people who helped make it possible.

Whenever I remember the day our daughter, Katie, was born, I think about standing in the hallway of the hospital all by myself. Moments before, we were in the midst of excitement and joy, when the monitor told the doctors that her heart rate had dropped dramatically.

Before I realized what was happening, they had rushed TJ into the operating room, leaving me alone. As I stood in that hallway, it was my faith that held me together. Somehow, I trusted that everything would be okay.

When a nurse came out of the operating room, she saw me and pulled me inside. I walked in just in time to see the doctor lift Katie into the world and a few moments later she was in my arms.

As I walked her toward the hospital nursery, I didn't realize how much she would be like me. Her willful nature and her competitive spirit are mirror images of mine. And, I didn't know that she would share my passion for running.

Twenty-seven months later, our son, Paul, was born. By all appearances, he was the perfect baby, scoring a ten on the Apgar test.

For a few days, all was well with our complete family. We had a "big sister party," an event that Paul slept through. After that, it didn't feel like he slept again for the next six months.

He screamed, a lot, and the doctors couldn't figure out what was wrong. Looking back now, I don't know how we survived with the meager amount of sleep we all got, not to mention the worry of knowing Paul was suffering.

After months of testing, an MRI finally showed reflux; Paul had heartburn. The doctor prescribed an alternating dose of Maalox and Mylanta, because one caused diarrhea and the other caused constipation.

The ultimate cure came when Paul began to sit up, which is when we finally saw his true self.

His smile alone could put me in a good mood. His laugh was happy music. He gave me back my boyish self, something I'd lost in the seriousness of life. For the first six years of Paul's life, half of his birthday and Christmas presents were really for me.

TJ and I immersed ourselves in family life, which is what most people do I guess, and the ensuing years gave us a collection of memories that have since become the shared possession we love more than any other.

Katie's search for independence began immediately. She was strong willed and sure of herself. Once school began, she was an achiever, never satisfied with anything less than her very best.

Paul's journey was different. He was a creator, using his imagination to build new realities. We'd find leprechaun traps in the corners of rooms and get invited to attend his grand events – puppet shows and the like.

It all seems so long ago now, especially when I spend time with the young adults my children have become. But when I connect the dots between now and then, I can see that they are simply larger and more mature versions of their child selves, which seems perfectly fitting. To me, they've always been perfect.

When I first started running with Katie, Paul wanted to start running too. I was cautious about having him begin too soon, but in time he would join us. In a lifetime of unforgettable running memories, those runs with my kids rise above all the others.

Both of my children would follow in my running footsteps, but for Paul, it was more of an activity than a sport. So, when he gave up high school track to be in a school play, I was happy to see him discover something he could feel more passionate about.

As a father, there have been many lessons I've tried to teach. I had a list of knowledge and experiences I wanted to transfer, but I'm afraid I've only been marginally successful. Life seems to teach better than I do.

There is something valuable, though, that I think my kids have gained from me: life is sweeter when you discover your passion, and then live it.

It was four o'clock on a Friday afternoon, and I decide to leave the pressure of the work week a little earlier than normal. I grabbed my running bag and walked towards the locker room in my office building.

I was celebrating a promotion, a milestone I didn't think I'd reach in my career, and a short run at the end of the workweek seemed like an appropriate self-indulgence.

As I began my run, I had no company on the pathway, except for the flock of geese that scattered as I approached. They flew to the middle of a large pond, and as they hit the icy water, I was glad I wasn't one of them.

I didn't have any particular route planned. Instead, I wandered from place to place. I ran past the track where I've done some of my hardest workouts and by the trail where I've found peace away from many hectic mornings.

I was running easy, trying to reflect on what I had just accomplished and in the middle of the run something unexpected occurred to me. My run wasn't as much a celebration as it was a tribute to the thing that has contributed more to my personal success than anything else I can name.

Based on my education and background, I've climbed higher up the corporate ladder than I ever should have, and I have the disciplines of running to thank for that.

I never once believed that someone or something else was responsible for my success. Running taught me long ago that there is danger in that kind of thinking. The moment you leave your future in the hands of things outside of your control, is the moment you place it in the hands of circumstance. And, circumstance doesn't much care about your success.

Running has also taught me that adversity is better faced head-on than avoided. The hill in front of you won't go away, but it's easy enough to put it behind you if just press harder for a while. Call it discipline, or call it determination, without it you won't get very far.

That lesson isn't taught enough, and too many people never realize that sacrifice is a requirement of life. You either sacrifice today to reach tomorrow's goals, or you give up your dreams in favor the fleeting comfort that's distracting you. The pleasant reality, for those who choose the former, is that comfort is abundant when long-term goals are achieved.

When my run was finished I went back inside and took a quick shower. I walked back to my office to grab my briefcase before heading home. I said goodbye wondering if anyone even noticed that I had been gone during my run.

The following Monday, when I arrived back at work, I looked outside my office window and saw the geese gathered around the pond. I watched them for a few moments before getting my day started.

As I went about my morning, I faced pressing challenges, gave guidance to the people around me and tried to create vision for what lies ahead.

Then, when lunchtime rolled around, I grabbed my running bag and spent some time strengthening the disciplines through which I've earned the privilege to do all those things.

Before the start of the 2015 Christie Clinic Illinois Marathon, Nick Agoris waited in the chilly gloom with a mass of runners

Nick is a coach, probably the premier independent shot-put coach in the mid-Atlantic region. He's mentored dozens of Maryland State High School Champions. And, in many cases, his direction has helped individuals receive scholarship awards that they never would have received without him. Nick changes lives.

We were teammates at South Carroll High School in the late 1970s. We were friends back then, but I can't say that we were close. Nick was a thrower, and I was a distance guy. We traveled in slightly different circles.

Today, we have a friendship I would have trouble explaining. It's similar to the bond you form after you've run beside a person for hundreds of miles, even though Nick and I never run together.

If you spent time with the two of us, you probably wouldn't observe a lot of similarities. Nick's outgoing. I'm more reserved. He's spirited. I'm not.

The commonalities lie underneath our personalities. Our coaching experiences have led us both to understand that the pathway to improved performance is relatively easy. Follow a proven approach and the gains will come.

Developing admirable qualities, on the other hand, is hard. Humility doesn't often join talent. A sense of urgency can kill patience.

Having lived the lives of aging athletes, Nick and I are beginning to understand the intricate balance needed to have success and well-being at the same time, and we've spent many lunchtime hours sharing what we've learned.

In classic Nick Agoris style, he wasn't in Illinois just to run the marathon. He set a goal to accomplish a feat that, to the best of everyone's knowledge, has never been done before. In the same weekend, he would attempt to bench press 300 pounds, throw a 16-pound shot-put twelve meters, and finish a marathon.

On Saturday, Nick struggled in his bench-press "warm up," just barely lifting 280 pounds. Concerned that he might only have one more good lift in him, he skipped 290 and made an attempt at 300, but he couldn't raise the bar.

The throwing didn't go well, and he closed the first day without reaching two of his three goals.

So he was waiting in the chilly gloom to run a marathon that had less meaning than it did twenty-four hours beforehand.

The weather forecast wasn't good. Light rain was falling twenty minutes after the start and it became steady by the time Nick reached mile four. By the eighth mile, he was trudging forward in an absolute downpour.

If you've never run in rain like that, it's a unique experience. Your vision is impaired. Puddles become ponds. An uncomfortable chill consumes you, and your only ally is disassociation.

Despite the heavy rain, Nick was running well. He reached mile eighteen feeling good, but given the events of the weekend to that point, he should have been prepared for something else to go wrong.

He first heard it over a police car intercom – severe storms were approaching and the course was being closed. Runners were told to board the buses that would be coming momentarily.

Nick, being the rebel that he is, didn't listen. He ran over to the sidewalk hoping the race officials wouldn't see him. He passed the nineteen mile marker and kept running, but when the next mile marker he saw was 24, he realized he'd missed a turn.

He ran to the finish line inside the University of Illinois stadium. There were still volunteers there to give Nick a finisher's medal, but he knew he was about four miles short of a marathon.

Before I finish the story, I should explain something. Nick's parents didn't have much. They worked hard, harder than most people are willing to work today, for every dollar they earned.

They never complained, never once made Nick or his brothers believe life wasn't fair. They simply did what they had to do, and they managed to be happy about it. Back then, values were worth more than material things.

Nick was cold, stiff and exhausted, but a marathon is 26.2 miles, and just like his parents did before him, Nick finishes what he starts.

He didn't have a GPS watch, but he decided that even his slowest shuffle would allow him to cover a mile in fifteen minutes. And so, he ran on the concrete walkway under the stadium, back and forth, for an hour.

"It's hard to go wrong in life if you do what you say you're going to do," Nick once told me.

We all appreciate reliability when we see it in someone else. But reliability's real worth comes when you can find it in yourself.

The next time we meet for lunch, I have a question for Nick: What's the single most important condition of happiness? I have an idea about what he'll say, but trust me, it will be fascinating conversation.

It was spitting outside, a term my mother used when I was young and the rain was so scant that you couldn't see it falling.

While spit may have a negative connotation to you, this was the Angels spitting, and so the drops were holy water.

I began my run with angel spit on my glasses.

It was early on a Sunday morning, and I shuffled in front of Westminster High School, my car parked in the empty lot behind me. If the run went as planned, I'd be doing ten miles, looping around the grounds that connected the high school with the YMCA.

The sun was covered by the hovering clouds and the air was humid. I was glad to be out before the day heated up.

I made my way around the far side of the school and then over to the track. On the first lap my Garmin watch buzzed, and I knew one mile was behind me. I didn't look at the watch.

I loped around the track for a while, my stride slowly beginning to move freely.

Thirty-six years before, my parents would have been in the stadium stands watching me run some of my final races as a South Carroll senior.

By then, they had taught me much of the wisdom I rely on today, and most of it can be summed up in the idioms they would use.

I never remember my mother losing her patience. I never remember her yelling. She simply repeated phrases that held the wisdom of the ages.

When I was impatient she'd say, "Hold your horses."
When I was fixated on something, she'd say, "Don't put
all your eggs in one basket." In time, I got the messages.

I finished my laps around the track and ran onto the grass
of the school yard. The drizzle had stopped by the time I
reached Washington Road, and I stayed on the grass as I
went by Robert Moton Elementary and onto the
grounds of the community college.

My father encouraged me to go to college, but I never
did, so I relied upon my early lessons as I began adult-
hood.

Once, after I had stayed home sick from school, my dad
came into my bedroom at the end of the day. It was the
third time in as many weeks that I had stayed home, and
there may have been some embellishment when I described how sick I was feeling.

He sat on the side of my bed and, for the first time, told
me the story about the boy who cried wolf. I wasn't sick
for the rest of that school year.

I ran onto the grounds of the YMCA where a gravel path
circles the grounds. By then, I was trying to remember all
the old sayings my parents used. I remember learning that
I should never "judge a book by its cover" and not to
"count your chickens before they hatch."

There were times when my faith was restored when I
realized that a disappointment could be "a blessing in
disguise."

As I ran the final loop around the gravel path, my watch
buzzed for the eighth time. I left the path and began
running back towards my car.

I don't know how many miles I've run over the years, but I do know that most of what I've learned about life was reinforced while I was running them.

Running isn't an avocation for the insincere. Talk won't prepare you for any race. "Actions speak louder than words," as my father would say.

And once a race is over, whether you achieved a goal or not, you should heed my mother's advice and accept the outcome because, by then, "it's water under the bridge."

My legs were heavy in the final mile, but my pace was steady. I stopped just before I reached the car and then walked up to the door. There was a drop on the window, angel spit. I wiped it with my finger and smiled.

Some people will tell you that our life is defined by the choices we make, and that may be partly true. But once a choice is made, the eternal principles of life preside over it.

My parents spoke the truth and running made it clear. In this life you get what you pay for, nothing more. Invest heavily.

March 2, 2003 was marked on my calendar far in advance. I was training for a marathon, and every run and workout was leading me toward that day.

The previous October I had mapped out my running schedule. Every detail was scripted.

The winter was a cold one. There were days when I wanted to stay inside where it was warm, but I resisted all the excuses. I ran what was scheduled each day, long runs, track workouts and tempo runs were all done as planned. I noted each workout in my log, but didn't care too much about them independently. They were just a part of something bigger.

The blizzard of 2003 came on February 16th. The B&A trail was covered with a couple feet of snow, too much to melt away in the cold temperatures that followed. It was upsetting to learn that the race was canceled.

I looked at the calendar when I woke up on March 2nd and stared at the note marking the big event. I looked at that note every day until we turned the calendar on April 1st.

It's not that I didn't benefit from the training. I did. In fact, that spring I ran some great races. It's just that none of them meant as much as the one I didn't run.

I've noticed that we tend to thrive on milestones and events. We look forward to the next big day and act like the days in between are obstructions we'd like to brush aside. My mother used to refer to that as wishing your life away. Now, I see her point.

My children are both young adults now. When each of them turned twenty-one, we thought of it as a milestone. I remember all the others as well, the events and the parties. I remember the holidays and family gatherings. We made those days special, and I'm glad we did.

Still, I'd like a do-over on some of the ordinary days, when nothing particularly special was happening.

I'd like the chance to put work aside so I could sit by my kids on the couch, watch whatever they were watching on TV, and feel their head resting on my shoulder. I'd like the chance to change my response when they told me they were bored, so that I could play whatever they wanted. I want to listen to the giggles that have since faded away and feel the touch of tiny hands that don't live here anymore.

I thrive on goals. And, once I set one, I always create a plan and do my best to follow it. But it's different now. I don't squander my time hoping a big day will come more quickly. I've done that before, and I realize now what's been lost along the way.

<u>Chapter 10:</u>

Self–acceptance

My body remembers every mile, even as my mind forgets them.

– Dave Griffin on Running

My running life is really a series of lives.

High school was the start of it. After I realized my slight frame wasn't going to get much playing time in other sports, I started running.

There was an acclimation period, a feeling out of sorts, but that didn't take long. I found out quickly that I was good at running, and the rules of the sport were easy to understand.

But life was complicated then, not that the world was any more or less crazy. Life is always distorted when seen through the eyes of a teenager, and I was no different than anyone else.

So I began running at a time when I was mostly confused, about life in general and my life in particular.

Running became my stability and my certainty. I confronted myself with challenges through running, and as I overcame them I learned that I could also handle the challenges I had little control over. The confidence felt good.

When school was finished, running became a meaningful choice. I could have easily given it up. I had no more teammates and no coach, but I decided running suited me. I liked the discipline. I liked the private battles running forced upon me, demanding that I either win or lose, but on terms I controlled.

I could define these as the glory years, a time of promise and accomplishment. But it was also a time of self-discovery, when I began to realize the heights of my potential. There were few restrictions, my body could withstand a heavy load, and I applied it regularly.

Based on my running logs, I ran about 130 races between 1982 and 1989, crossing the finish line first forty-two times.

The final win of those years came on June 11, 1989. The notes in my log simply memorialized the race and my time. I didn't make any detailed comments.

If I had known the significance of the race, I would have appreciated it more. I'd remember every detail, the competition, the weather, the course. I'd remember how it felt to cross the finish line and the afterglow of my cool down.

"Life is made up of meetings and partings, that is the way of it," said Kermit the Frog in The Muppets Christmas Carol. I wish I had recognized that parting.

There was a long phase after that, when I offered running less of myself. Other priorities capitalized my time, so I would run when I could, but it was without any real purpose or expectation.

These were the years when running became an escape from busy life. Whenever I needed it, running offered a peacefulness that was hard to find elsewhere.

I had a brief surge of competitiveness in my early forties. I must have heard the clock ticking, so I rekindled the old feelings, pushed again through hard workouts, and rediscovered my love of the sport.

And then came this phase, when my body doesn't always cooperate with my ambition. It has been a period of reflection as I finally begin to realize how this journey has gifted me so.

What Kermit the Frog failed to say is this: Between the meeting and the parting is where life is lived.

My body remembers every mile, even as my mind forgets them. My fiber was built through the rigor, my motivation born in the passion. I will always know what it feels like to push through a formidable obstacle and get to the other side.

I know how being alone should feel, and it isn't lonely. I've discovered a peacefulness that few in this world can describe. And while running has led me on this path of discovery, I realize now that the serenity is in my own heart.

I have been blessed by those who ran beside me. They have moved me to my greatest moments and supported me in my hardest grief. They have loved and inspired me every step of the way.

I am at a stage now when I can fully rely upon my values and beliefs, not with a certainty that would assert my perspective on someone else, but in a way that allows my heart to trust the way it feels.

There has been purpose to it all, I know it. Every meeting and parting has moved me in a direction that I needed to go, even if I didn't always choose it.

And some day, when I finally reach a level of enlightenment that has thus far eluded me, I will understand how all these pieces fit together, moving me closer to becoming the man I need to be.

The written word reveals something to the writer. So in the years that I've been writing, I've learned some things about myself.

Now I'm on a quest, wondering where my own words might eventually lead me. Those of you who faithfully read my writing may be searching too, and we could all be looking for the same elusive thing.

I have to begin with some of my earliest memories, when I was a boy playing sports in my back yard. Always the youngest and smallest, I needed to prove that I was capable of competing with the others.

A child's imagination is a powerful thing, so I don't know how much of my memory is real. I recall being overwhelmed and overpowered, but I also remember exciting moments, times when I believed that I could compete with anyone.

While the joy of boyhood was written on our faces, there was something serious about the games we played. In the nearby city, legends threw touchdown passes and hit home runs. I dreamed of becoming one of them.

And as I compared my own capabilities to those of the boys around me, athleticism became a measuring stick.

It's no wonder that when I began running in high school there was nothing casual about it. I spotted the best runners in the area and set out on a pursuit to become one of them. There were victories back then, but not enough to satisfy my craving. So when I skipped college and got a job, I wasn't ready to give it up.

I spent the next ten years training hundreds of hours for every few moments of satisfaction that came from crossing a finish line first. The satisfaction never lasted. It always seemed like I could have run faster. There was always another runner I wanted to beat.

I imagine most good athletes are wired in a similar way. Contentment and diligence don't often mingle.

It's been forty years since I ran my first race. The world is immeasurably changed, and so is the body in which I reside. Nevertheless, I can't seem to douse the competitive ember. So when I run, especially on good days, that old desire comes again.

There are good things about that. Running fast feels natural. Enduring the pain of fatigue for the sake of improvement feeds my heart, but I'm beginning to recognize an underlying feeling that doesn't.

I have a friend who wanted to hear my running story, so I told him. When I was finished, there was a pause before he spoke. Then he used a word to describe how I sounded, and it took me a moment to hear it – disappointed.

I would have disagreed if he hadn't been right. The goals I didn't reach, the races I failed to win, the rivals I couldn't catch all still disappoint me.

I'm living with this illusion that I can still run a race that would cure my regret. If I could only train long and hard enough, new achievements might overshadow my perception of the past.

But what my friend said next shocked me into reality. "Someday, you're going to have to give it up."

A part of this seems so silly. I feel selfish for belittling my running achievements when so many others would love to own them. I feel ashamed that I still measure myself with race times that no one else cares about.

So, I'm on a quest to find the virtue we all desperately need – self-acceptance.

It's an internal journey. But whenever I put my thoughts down on paper I create something tangible to guide me.

I want to run just because it brings me joy. I want to run fast because I love the feeling. And whether I'm relaxed on a quiet trail or suffering in the final stages of a race, I want to enjoy the miles I have left without condition.

Ed Powelson was the athletic director at North Carroll High School for decades. In 1988 he graciously allowed me to coach the cross-country team there. I'm not a teacher, I had no coaching experience, and I was just twenty-seven years old.

I don't know if he had any reservations about letting me coach. If he did, he didn't show it.

You didn't have to be around Ed for long to realize that he put his heart into the school's athletic program. He was a man of principle. His passion rubbed off on me, and I wanted to do my best to represent the school because I knew I was also representing him.

At that point, most of what I knew about running is what I'd learned through my own experiences. First, success in racing requires hard work. Second, most high school kids will avoid hard work if possible.

To assure that everyone on the team worked hard, I ran many of the workouts with them. There were few opportunities to goof off. They ran farther than they had ever run, and they were pushed in different ways.

As the season progressed I could see the team getting

better, and by the time the championship races rolled around, we were contenders. We steamrolled the other teams in the regional race, taking three of the top four places. And then the team won the state title by a margin of sixty-three points.

Back in 1988, I was too young to appreciate the affect Ed had on me, but when I heard that he'd passed on, I closed my eyes and silently acknowledged his influence. Despite not having seen him for twenty-five years, it hurt knowing he was gone.

After I stopped coaching at North Carroll, I don't recall going to another cross-country meet until September 5, 2003. It was a beautiful fall day. The air was fresh and there was a slight breeze, so you could feel the coolness.

Katie, had decided to run cross-country the summer before her freshman year at Winters Mill High School. I was probably happier than I should have been.

When I arrived to watch the twenty-team meet, I saw the make-shift camp sites scattered around, and I walked the fields talking with people I knew.

I first saw Katie after her team finished the course walk. I wanted to run up and hug her, to let her know how excited I was, but by then I had learned the important parental virtue of self-restraint.

As the teams lined up, I walked out so I could get a good look at the start. In the sprint from the line, Katie bumped into one of her teammates, Roxanne Fleischer. She turned to Roxanne and laughed. That's when I knew she would be fine.

I ran out to the mid-point of the race and saw Katie running in a small pack of girls not far behind the leaders. Then I ran back to watch the finish.

As runners began to pass me, I counted. Katie came by me looking strong in thirteenth place.

Afterwards, all I wanted to do was find her. I saw her sharing the moment with her teammates, so I kept my distance for a short time, then I rushed over, gave her a hug and said, "Oh my gosh." She laughed.

I've read that important people in our lives are here to help guide us along our way. They show us possibilities and gently encourage us to take the right path. It's never forceful, just a loving nudge that we are free to accept, or not, on our own terms.

The summer after her freshman year, Katie inspired me to start the Flying Feet Running Programs. At the time, there was no structured running program to help local kids get ready for cross-country in the fall.

Eleven runners joined in the summer of 2004 – Katie, nine of her teammates, and Paul. The following fall, Katie's team, in just the third year in school history, finished second at the Maryland State meet.

Today, Flying Feet isn't anything like it used to be. It's evolved as I've gained experience and the dynamics of the group have changed, but I often remember the meager beginning.

My running could have been a selfish pursuit, my life an unconscious drifting. Thankfully, Ed Powelson did his best to show me and, years later, Katie gave me a gentle reminder - we are here to share something of ourselves.

Important messages are often found in the silence of isolated trails, where we can hear the wisdom of those who've run beside us. Make sure you're listening.

We lived in the house where our children grew up for almost twenty years. It was new when we bought it, and after years of nesting there it became a reflection of ourselves.

Katie and Paul were little when we moved in, and we started a tradition of notching a wooden post in the basement to mark their growth. We made the first marks on May 8, 1994. I don't remember anything else about that date, but two red lines tell me it was a special day.

Those were the years of noisy excitement, when squeals and laughter rattled through the house like the forced air heat. TJ and I joined in the play until we became too exhausted, and then we observed the kid's endurance with admiration.

Those were years of priceless quiet too, when wet hair rested on my arm after bath time and before I carried my children upstairs to bed, one at a time in the years after they became too heavy for me to carry them both together.

I miss the quiet moments most of all, the times when one of my children would cuddle beside me, simply to enjoy the closeness.

A mark on the post tells me that Katie was 4'10" when we began running together, a mile through the neighborhood at first, and then gradually longer. Running was our special time, when the boundaries between our generations dissolved and she offered a larger glimpse into her life.

For a few years, the two of us shared our competitive passion, each trying to get the most from ourselves in races. It became an honored connection between the two of us.

The last mark on the post was made in February of 2007 after Paul turned sixteen. Two years beforehand, he had gained bragging rights as our tallest child.

When we decided to sell that home, most everything was left behind, except for one thing – a wooden post.

The continuum of my life has started to change. What used to be endless seasons pass by in weeks, and I can't recall most of the days that fill the gap between now and my hazy youth.

There are times when I wish I had marked more moments, like the ones on the post. But then I remember how memories dissolve in time. It is the feelings that last.

We should all live life in a way that makes us feel good, not a fleeting, selfish good, but one that plants an enduring stillness that we can hold while life speeds away.

I've already forgotten nearly every mile I've run, but that's okay. Running makes me feel good, and it leaves behind comfort that lingers, like dampness on my sleeve from a sleepy child's wet hair.

Every journey ends. Sometimes, you even reach your destination.

In the mid to late 1980s, my destination, as I dreamed it, was an Olympic Trials qualifying marathon, a standard set at two hours and twenty minutes at the time.

None of my performances pointed to that kind of potential. My best PR, a 32:11 10K, predicted only a 2:29 marathon, so my goal had a measure of reverie about it.

My first two attempts to run a good marathon didn't go well and after a disappointing Marine Corp finish in 1985, I decided to put off another attempt for a while.

I focused on other race distances, setting short-term goals that I thought could become stepping stones towards a better marathon.

Those goals became journeys in and of themselves. I mapped out training plans and followed them faithfully. I increased the volume and intensity of my training along the way and achieved many of the goals I set for myself.

By 1988 I was racing better at the half marathon distance, and while nothing I accomplished predicted that I was ready to run a trails qualifying marathon, the dream kept me motivated.

I raced well in the spring of 1989 and planned to make another attempt at the marathon that fall, but by the time the year ended my competitive days were over, my journey unfinished.

Dave Kartalia's journey ended on March 11, 2015. He was surrounded by the people he most loved and died peacefully.

I knew Dave as a runner in the 1980s. Like so many of us back then, he used running as a way to test himself, and he became good at it.

He was a lawyer by trade, a good one, providing skilled and valued counsel.

But that's not where his intellect began or ended. Dave was a reader and a lover of music. He captured deep meaning in words and melody. He spoke many languages, some fluently, and used it as a way to learn about diverse cultures.

And he was a lover of nature as much as of ingenuity. He was a skilled fisherman and grew a garden that few could duplicate.

When his family spoke at his service, they mentioned a long list of remarkable accomplishments. In the words of his children – "he lived fiercely."

But they also spoke about the deep relationship they shared with Dave. And as I listened, it became clear to me that his greatest attribute had nothing to do with what he did or what he knew. It was his ability to love others and influence them in a positive way.

In his lifetime, Dave was a mentor, a coach, a listener and a confidant. He was a companion and a guide. Even in his final hours, he was teaching those around him how to live without inhibition and die without fear.

Dave was a man who reached his destination.

This life is complicated. Anyone who tells you that they've figured it out hasn't. But people like Dave can help us in our own meager attempts to understand it more fully.

We should challenge ourselves, absolutely. We should set goals with a certain amount of reverie. We should try to satisfy our curiosity about the world and about our place in it.

In the process we'll learn. We will grow stronger.

Success is likely to follow. We'll become accomplished. And, if our motives are just, we'll grow comfortable with ourselves so that we can begin to place our attention on someone else.

I know now what I couldn't understand before. A running goal isn't a destination - it's a catalyst.

My own running potential is a shadow of what it once was. As I run now, my patience is tested more than my endurance. My running times don't improve, but my ability to empathize does. Maybe that's the point.

I'm not at Dave's noble level, almost no one is, but his example is the destination we should all be seeking.

Fiercely pursue the things that feed your heart. The pursuit will create you.

But, even more, be aware that a day will come when those you've loved will rise and reminisce about the way you made them feel. In the end, that's how our journey will be measured.

Chapter 11:

A divine stillness

Underneath the cacophony that we've somehow learned to live with, is a divine stillness.

– Dave Griffin on Running

Peace

In the earliest days of my life, I had peace. I didn't need to prove anything. I didn't need to achieve anything. All I had to do was be myself.

The truth is, that's all I've ever needed to be. Once that became clear, I could stop struggling and simply be true to myself.

I know what the breeze feels like, a fast breeze self-manufactured with a stride that swallows pavement. I've felt it all at once from head to foot while it rushed behind me and whispered in my ears.

I remember how it feels to drift effortless along the ground with a mind settled on a single, nearly unconscious thought – relax. I can still feel a body as synergized as dancers on a Broadway stage, every part working in fluid unison.

And as the ground sped by in the flowing swiftness, I remember the stillness inside me, like a passenger in a speeding train, quietly enjoying the ride.

There were times when I was sure I could run as fast and as far as I wanted. Once, several miles into a ten-mile training run, it started on a long, down-hill stretch. It felt like my body was working under anesthesia while my mind stayed wide awake; I was floating.

And there were times when I was leading a race, so in control of the final result that I could simply enjoy the experience. I would run alone, knowing the others were behind me and feeling like my small body was more powerful than the strongest bricklayer.

I was young then, unaware of the thief that takes things from you while you're not paying attention, things you loved but never fully appreciated.

Back then, an aging future was like a myth, something I'd heard about but didn't think I'd see myself.

Time is the swift runner now, moving by so fast that I can never see him in the blur. He lives without the laws of the human body, moving faster with every year he acquires even when I'm sure he could never accelerate more.

I was on vacation in a location where I fish on an old, wooden pier. I'm usually alone there, and I've noticed something special about the place; time hasn't found it yet. And so I used the chance to close my eyes, relive some glorious moments, and honor them in the only appropriate way – graciously.

Time will eventually force each one of us to learn how to let something go; we have to teach ourselves how to do it willingly.

If you're struggling with that, find a place untouched by time and meditate on what you've been missing, not to pine a loss but to embrace what you've gained from the blessing. Gratitude is a freeing virtue even when its expression is delayed.

We acquire wisdom at the same pace in which we're ready to receive it.

As I mused on that old pier, the breeze gifted me a whisper in my ears, and I finally heard a message I've been ignoring for far too long - joy lies not in an able body, but in a spirit that's free to accept it. Mine is.

There's a quiet cove at Liberty Reservoir, where a large rock rest along the shoreline. When I was a boy, I used to fish off that rock. I remember sitting there with my line in the water, watching, and waiting for a tug. My father was nearby, fishing himself, but ready to help if I happened to catch anything.

The peacefulness of those experiences stay with me. Even today, all I have to do it cast my line, and I feel relaxed.

I'm not very good at fishing; I've never learned to use lures. I simply tie on a hook, add a worm, and then wait, sometimes for a very long time.

My daughter, Katie, and I were looking for a shady place to run, somewhere away from the June sun, so we drove to Liberty Reservoir to run on the fire trails there. Just as we started, we went by the old rock, still looking like it did forty years ago.

The trail was just as I remembered it too, except for the hills, which are more significant to a runner than they are to a fisherman.

It had been a while since we'd run together. The last time, we were both training to accomplish some goal, so there was a competitive purpose to the run. This time, that was absent; it was just she and I, together, doing something we both love to do.

We even stopped a few times, exploring one thing or another. Once, she thought she saw a spider, so we went back to search, only to find a trail of large, black ants marching somewhere. Katie told me how ants travel long distances to search, and then incredibly find their way back home again.

Eventually we turned around ourselves, having run out as far as we wanted. We never saw another soul, the entire trail was ours, and the joy that came from sharing the solitude would be impossible to describe; I needed that time with her.

Before, I had been in a pensive mood, impacted by the changes of life and the struggles of the world. While we were together, none of that mattered.

It's not going to change, you know. All you have to do is read the pages of history to learn that there has always been strife. I expect there always will be, in one form or another. But, there will also be places beyond the grasp of human nature and bad news, where a runner can leave all that behind, if only for a time.

When our run was over, we walked along the trail, exploring the lake for a while longer before we left.

Years from now, I imagine she'll return to run passed the old rock and along the quiet cove. She'll leave her troubles behind, and think about how it all looks so familiar.

The world seemed big around the deserted back road where I was running.

To my left mountains loomed, forming a barrier between me and the distance beyond. They made me feel small as I moved through the ninth mile of a twelve mile run.

In the space between me and the mountains, there was a quiet valley, asleep from the cold air that had lingered in recent weeks. A wide stream passed through. Without it, the place would have been dormant. Nothing else moved, except for me.

There was a forest to my right. It was in hibernation too; the shades of brown gave it a peaceful, yet lifeless look.

Ahead of me the road went on forever, only disappearing beyond the crest of a hill. I was alone on that road; I hadn't seen another person since the run began. I felt a fatigue only a runner can understand. Within it there was strength, an understanding that I was many miles away from complete exhaustion.

I had started to pick up my pace a mile or so before. On a longer run, effort needs to be rationed in the early miles but spent more freely later on. I felt good, the rhythm relaxing me. The only sounds were those of my own movement.

I climbed the hill in front of me knowing I had just a couple miles left to run. At the crest, I could see an old farm house surrounded by still cattle and a big pond not yet covered by winter ice. A single cow stood by the road, and we watched each other as I ran by her.

When I'm running life is simple. Workloads and deadlines never cross my mind. Worry is absent. There is no need for money or some gadget to make things more convenient.

When I'm running I don't need to know the latest news; turmoil and tragedy are far away. If some crisis is brewing, I'm unaware. It isn't that running lets me abandon my responsibility; it just frees me of the burden for a time.

When I'm running the only relationship that matters is the one I have with myself. After so many hours of private effort, I've grown fond of my time alone, and there's something important about that.

I know that my own stamina and fortitude will always be enough. There is no hill too steep. There is no bad stretch that won't end. No matter how big the world around me may seem, any challenge can be overcome inside my own determination.

The final mile was just as peaceful as the others. I moved through a bend in the road and saw my car parked off in the distance. I ran just passed it to reach twelve miles and then slowly walked back.

I stretched and drank some water before driving off, leaving behind less than I carried away.

❧

The music from the boom-box was too loud for me to lay so close to it, but I didn't care.

It was the end of indoor track practice in the winter of 1979. We had a big meet the following day, and someone had brought the music to relax the mood. When I was done with my light workout, I walked over and lay down in front of it.

The rest of the team milled around the gym, some of them still making final preparations for the next day, but I closed my eyes and forgot they were even there.

Back then, music was like a reset button. I could get lost in it, feel the emotions I was suppressing beneath my teenage facade, acknowledge the sometimes painful reality they represented, and then let them roll away.

I don't remember what songs played. I don't know who thought I was strange for lying there. All I know is, for whatever amount of time I lay listening, the unsettled world was peaceful.

The next day, when the gun sounded for the 1,000 meters, I sprinted off the line with the rest of the leaders. The distance was short for me, but I was motivated by the deadlines enforced by my senior year.

By the time we reached the last two laps of the 200 meter track, I was already at a full sprint, so when the ultimate winner began to pull ahead, I was left to race to second place. Even so, up to that point in my running life, it was the best race I'd run.

Becoming a runner in high school was a turning point for me. I was shy, too quiet to allow myself to be heard by anyone but my closest friends. There was an uncertainty about me; I didn't know how to fit myself into the puzzle of adolescence.

Running gave me certainty. It gave me permission to be myself.

Still, there was a fierceness about running back then. It was sport, plain and simple, and I approached it that way.

So, when I needed peace, I turned on the music and found it in the blaring sound.

Peace comes to me in silence now, in the muffled rhythm of motion.

I often wonder how anyone lives without having a

peaceful escape. Life can be wearing, pushing you ever further away from the harmony you're seeking.

As we get older, some people forget what it feels like to be tranquil, to have settled emotions, or to be comfortable with what's going on inside them.

It doesn't have to be that way. Underneath the cacophony that we've somehow learned to live with, is a divine stillness.

TJ and I love our vacation weeks in Lewes, Delaware, a small beach town with a unique history and quiet water.

Before one of our trips there, I told a friend that I really needed to get away. For some reason, the normal challenges had seemed considerably harder than normal.

I'm not really sure what had changed. Work was the same, the unique blessing of security combined with the burden of needing to support the things I'm responsible for. All in all, I'm more fortunate than most, but that doesn't mean it isn't hard sometimes.

But the challenges were coming one after another, and I looked forward to stepping away from all of that, if only for nine days.

When I'm on vacation, life isn't scripted. I let days lead where they may, never worrying much about time. The only thing normal about my routine is running.

But even my runs weren't the same. I never found the normal spark of energy. It seems without the stress of work there's nothing to ignite it, no steam to blow off, and my runs are more sedate.

I found myself looking for places to stop and explore. I ran to the Cape Henlopen State Park, where a bike trail circles drifting dunes. There's a spot where you can look out over the ocean, and I'd watch dolphins swimming up the shoreline. There must have been dozens, all playfully swimming, and I wondered what it would be like to be one of them.

Cape Henlopen was a military base in the middle of the twentieth century, until long range missiles made the fort obsolete. I stopped to investigate the abandoned bunkers, and tried to imagine what I would have seen there in the 1940s.

Life is so different now. We have luxuries designed to simplify our life, but our lives aren't simple. We live in abundance, and yet we wrestle with desire. We take vacations to flee from things that are inescapable.

Before I finished each run, I'd go to the end of a deserted fishing pier and look past the lighthouses in the Delaware Bay. Life seems different when viewed from a new observation point.

This world is a beautiful place. Our life here, in no small measure, will be as good as we decide it will be.

You can't escape your obligations. You can run away, but guilt and new responsibility will soon find you.

So do what you must and do it well. Then, every day, spend time doing something deeply personal. It may not change your life, but it will change your perspective about it.

Chapter 12:

A beautiful place

Finally, where I'm going seems less important than where I am.

– Dave Griffin on Running

The trees seemed brittle, but restful. The earth looked dead and yet so much at peace. Leaves lay on the brown grass, an offering of sustenance to the fields that would be reborn soon enough. I ran along a pathway, immersed in the calmness.

The initial shock of cold made the early minutes uncomfortable, but that didn't last. The stiffness I always feel lingered longer than usual, but then eased away. I was running freely in a place I love being.

Winter running is the most isolated. Hibernation is widespread. Insects are gone, along with the people. The scarce birds are more visible, but also more quiet.

Solitude is an unappreciated gift. As I moved along the still pathway, I was free to exist simply. Gone was all pretense and obligation.

If someone had appeared in the distance, my pace would have quickened. A stranger, one I had not met and would not see again, would affect my posture. For reasons I can't explain, appearances would matter. It's silly, but it's also true.

No stranger appeared; I was alone for the entire run.

For a while, my troubles stayed with me. I thought about work and money. I thought about plans and people. My life, at this moment, entertained my mind with questions and answers. Some problems were solved.

But even the thoughts left me alone in time. My uncluttered mind floated along in the motion, and my body just carried my spirit along. I know words can't describe the feeling. Only those who've been there understand. The freeness and the clarity were indefinable.

The pathway I was on led to the foot of a high hill, and I began to climb. My frosted breath got heavy, and I labored around the bends. The rocks made me concentrate on my footfalls until I finally reached the top.

I stopped there, wanting to enjoy the feeling and the place. I could see for miles and spent some time looking into the distance. Then I turned my attention to closer things.

There was no wind to make a sound. If there was anything alive there, I didn't see it. I was far away from everything, except myself; I was closer to that than I have ever been.

I've run through a hundred seasons and watched the land adjust each time. It never seems burdensome, the change is natural. There is newness, followed by exuberance, followed by brilliance, and then - stillness.

We are a part of nature too, though we don't give it much thought. We enjoy the phases of life until we begin to fear the winter; we don't want to become brittle like a cold, leafless tree.

As I ran back, I felt synergy between myself and the land. We shared peacefulness, and I carried it home.

Even as I age and my body becomes frail, I will return to the sleeping pathway for winter runs, and reconnect with my ageless spirit.

The best runs feel effortless, which probably sounds kind of funny if you don't run. Running is supposed to be hard and even hurt sometimes, but I didn't feel any of that in the early miles of my long run.

I had just passed the seventh mile heading out to mile eight where I planned to turn around and run back the way I had come. I didn't feel much of anything, except relaxation. I was numb in the rhythm, hypnotized by the motion.

It wasn't that I was running slowly. I was moving faster than I had hoped. Of course, I had to overcome the choppiness of the early miles. The first few strides are the worst. Those feel uncomfortable, like when I first step from the bed in the morning and limp towards the bathroom.

There was a merciful break in the cold winter temperatures and I was running on some beautiful roads near Gettysburg. Maybe those things helped, but you never really know how a run is going to feel until it's underway.

I'm not sure my wife, TJ, understands much of this, even after living with me for so many years. I try not to explain it, satisfied with the simple blessing of knowing that she accepts me unconditionally.

There's a difference between falling in love and being in love and it seems like all the glamour is in the former. Enduring devotion is underappreciated by Hollywood, but not by me.

As I approached the eighth mile, I saw TJ's hand holding the Gatorade bottle out the car window. She asked how I was doing and I told her I was feeling good, took a drink and started running back knowing where I'd see her next.

You might say that we fit the definition of an old, married couple. There is a comfortable peace between the two of us, each of us knowing that we give something the other desperately needs. She needs my reason and stability. I need her warmth and support. The burden of life is easier because we carry it together.

My pace was even faster on the way back. I was immersed in the pure blessing of it all, not even thinking about how many miles were behind or in front of me.

I came around a turn and the car was there, just as I knew it would be. TJ smiled and handed me the bottle.

I ran the last few miles in firm concentration. The fatigue I was expecting never really came; it felt like I could have run forever.

When I was done, I stretched by the car while TJ waited patiently. I climbed in as she told me she enjoyed the quiet time while I was running. It let her see some places she hadn't seen before and get some reading done while the car was parked. If you want to know the truth, though, I think she came mostly because we enjoy each other's company.

The value of a relationship is in knowing that you are a better person because of it. Without her, I could have never come so far.

The wet air had settled like a cloud resting in the field across the street. I studied it for a moment and then walked down the driveway.

After a few quick drills, I started running, clunky with the morning stiffness. It was five-thirty; my body and my brain weren't synchronized yet. I ran up the first long hill in my new neighborhood, knowing I'd find a better rhythm at the top of it.

We moved to a new house just months before. It's our first post-kids home, the first time we've organized a house around our own selfish needs. There's only one bed, from which the laundry is just a few steps away, and the place flows in a way that's comfortable with our routines.

It's bright; the windows welcome the light, and the light obliges with a day-long dance upon our walls. One of the windows, in the room where I sit writing, gives a broad view of the field across the street, where you could have seen the hazy cloud resting, and me shuffling up the hill.

Our neighborhood is a series of looping streets. I made my way around the first one, finally feeling relaxed as I ran back by the house and into the next, longer loop.

I've never been a morning runner; this is something different for me. I've always preferred mid-day and evening runs, when I'm wide awake and more limber.

When I was in my twenties, I'd often sleep through the alarm, leaving my training buddies to start without me. They were as serious as they were friendly, so there was never a chance that they would start late. I would have to rush to catch up or keep sleeping and run alone.

I'm changing, I guess everything is, and suddenly pre-dawn seems like the perfect time for easy runs now that I'm running regularly again after an injury-force break.

Starting over is hard, although it's getting easier since I've done it so many times. There's the challenging first weeks when my body resists the activity, but my body re-acclimates as soon as it recognizes persistence.

The sun, sharing color with the horizon, made its appearance as I ran on the far side of the neighborhood. I moved away from it and back toward the house, before turning to run up the hill that begins a final loop.

I've started to think about what running means to me at this point in my life, about where I hope it takes me this time. There are twinges of deep desire leading to ambitious dreams. I want to feed those.

But of all the desires that live in me now, the most enduring is the want for peace, the kind of peace that lives in the morning before the world wakes up.

I finished my run and walked up to the house, a beautiful place in a beautiful time. Finally, where I'm going seems less important than where I am.

About the Author

Dave Griffin began running in 1976 as a high school freshman. He ran competitively through 1989 with PRs that include a 25:43 5M, a 32:11 10K and a 1:12:24 half marathon. In 1986, much the medial meniscus was removed during surgery to repair a non-running injury. The doctor advised Dave to stop running, warning that he would get arthritis if he continued. He returned to running and racing after the surgery, running some of his best races in 1987-89.

After a 12-year period of casual running when his children were young, he returned to competitive running as a master.

The doctor's warning came true in 2005, when Dave developed arthritis in his right knee. The years since have been riddled with injury, including a stress fracture in his right medial condyle while training for the 2012 Boston Marathon.

Dave started the Flying Feet Running Programs in 2004 while his daughter, Katie, was running in high school. The program has since grown to provide year-round coaching and support to runners of all experience and talent levels in the Carroll County, Maryland, area.

Dave begin writing about running and life in 2006, when his bi-weekly column, *Dave Griffin on Running,* was introduced. In 2010, Dave published his first book, *After the Last PR – The Virtues of Living a Runner's Life.*

You can find Dave on the internet at www.flyingfeetrunning.com
You can also find pages for his books on Facebook.

Made in the USA
Lexington, KY
14 November 2017